Cooking with Goodwill

Cooking
with
Goodwill

Goodwill Industries
of Delaware & Delaware County, Inc.

Library of Congress Control Number: 2003111075
ISBN #: 1-58320-051-7

Goodwill Industries of Delaware & Delaware County, Inc.
300 East Lea Boulevard
Wilmington, DE 19802

Printed in the United States
First printing September 2003
10 9 8 7 6 5 4 3 2 1

Table of Contents

Appetizers ... 12

Salads ... 26

Soups ... 38

Entrees ... 50

Pastas ... 82

Side Dishes ... 90

Desserts ... 104

Brunch ... 134

This and That ... 146

Index ... 155

Board and Administrative Team

Our Mission

The mission of Goodwill Industries
of Delaware & Delaware County, Inc.
is to improve the quality of life
for people with barriers to employment
through vocational services and work opportunities.

Your donations go right to work.

A Dash of History...

In 1902, Rev. Edgar J. Helms, a Methodist minister, began going door-to-door collecting used household goods and clothing in Boston, Massachusetts. He then trained and hired the poor and immigrants to mend and repair the used goods, which were resold. His original intent was to put people to work collecting, repairing, and reselling clothing and household items so they might experience the dignity of self-sufficiency.

Rev. John H. Beauchamp, a minister at the Asbury Methodist Church, visited Boston and was impressed with Rev. Helms' philosophy of "a hand up, not a hand out." In 1921, Goodwill Industries of Delaware & Delaware County was the six-teenth Goodwill to be incorporated — making it the oldest nonprofit 501© (3) providing vocational services in the state of Delaware.

A Pinch of Pride ...

Goodwill Industries of Delaware & Delaware County, Inc. is part of a network of 207 independent, community-based organizations in the U.S., Canada, and 22 other countries. Over the past 100 years, Goodwill Industries has provided employment, training, and rehabilitation services to over 5 million individuals with disabilities and other disadvantages, such as welfare dependency, homelessness, and lack of education or work experience. Goodwill strengthens the community by taking the "whole family" approach to workplace success; helping to provide the resources people need to obtain and maintain employment and help solve other family issues that prevent workers from being successful.

A Dollop of Success...

Locally, Goodwill Industries continues the tradition of recycling donated items through its award-winning thrift stores, Computer Recycling Center, and auctions. Although Goodwill Industries no longer repairs furniture or clothing or mends old shoes, Goodwill provides job training designed to give individuals marketable skills that meet the needs of today's businesses, such as food service training and computer skills training. And Goodwill continues to provide job opportunities. In addition to Goodwill thrift stores, Goodwill Industries operates a janitorial service, a staffing service, and an industrial contracts service – all designed to provide more jobs for more people and generate more revenue to support more Goodwill training programs. The result? Goodwill Industries proudly employs over 400 individuals – 70-85% of whom have a disability or other barrier to employment.

Following this 100-year-old recipe for success, with Goodwill Industries' help, people once relying on government assistance can experience the dignity of earning a paycheck and contributing to the economic vitality of the community.

Thank you ...

for purchasing Goodwill Industries of Delaware & Delaware County's cookbook. By purchasing this book, you are not only receiving wonderful recipes, but you are also helping to improve the lives of individuals with disabilities and other disadvantages. The proceeds from this book directly support Goodwill Industries' quality job-training programs for people with barriers to employment. As you read through this cookbook, you will find some interesting facts and information from the beginnings of Goodwill in Boston, Massachusetts, to the programs and services we offer today.

We would like to commend the committee of employees and volunteers that has made this publication possible. In particular, we would like to recognize Bob Older and Charles "Ebbie" Alfree III for their dedication and service to Goodwill. Bob and the committee worked extremely hard to collect scrumptious recipes from premier chefs in the area, local celebrities, and friends of Goodwill to bring you a one-of-a-kind collection of outstanding dishes with a hometown touch. Ebbie as Community Relations Manager pulled everything together and worked tirelessly with the committee and the publisher to ensure that we produced a quality product. Whether you want to impress your friends by creating a six-course meal or a satisfying, but quick salad for one, this book has a recipe for you.

It seems some of the most memorable times that we have spent with our families and friends have been in the kitchen cooking evening meals and holiday dinners. We hope you will create fond memories with your loved ones as you prepare delicious menus from this cookbook.

Bon Appetite,

Elaine Burg

Elaine Burg
Co-Chair, PR/Fundraising Committee

Karen Carello Nocket

Karen Carello Nocket
Co-Chair, PR/Fundraising Committee

Ted Van Name

Ted Van Name
President/CEO

Foreword

As a proud sponsor of Goodwill Industries of Delaware & Delaware County, Inc., I am honored to write the foreword to their cookbook. Every day, Goodwill Industries is strengthening families, providing opportunities, and improving the lives of individuals with barriers to employment through vocational services and work opportunities.

In an effort to raise funds for their quality job training programs, Goodwill Industries, among other fundraisers, decided to publish this book, which includes fabulous recipes and information regarding Goodwill's history and current programs and services. The book will serve as both a resource for preparing delectable meals and discovering the impact Goodwill has had in our region. The purchase of this book will help a mother feed her children, a father keep a house for his family, and all men and women feel the dignity of earning a paycheck, not depending on a handout.

As a restaurateur, I have met world-renowned chefs, dined at the most exquisite restaurants, and have read award-winning cookbooks. I am honored to be part of the growth of Goodwill Industries and be able to support the worthwhile businesses that Goodwill Industries of Delaware & Delaware County, Inc. have created to help people work. Goodwill Industries works so people can. The cookbook works so you can!

Enjoy!

Xavier Teixido
Owner, Harry Savoy Grill and Ballroom

Appe

NOT CHARITY, BUT A CHANCE!

tizers

Chipped Beef Dip

Kristin Strouss
Goodwill Staff

1 11-ounce package dried chipped beef
8 ounces cream cheese
½ cup sour cream
1 tablespoon milk
¼ cup chopped bell pepper
2 tablespoons onion flakes
1 teaspoon garlic powder

Preheat oven to 350º. Mix all ingredients together and place in an ovenproof serving dish. Bake for 20 minutes. Serve with crackers.

Serves 10 to 15
Complexity: Easy

About Goodwill

Goodwill was founded in 1902 in Boston's South End by the Reverend Edgar J. Helms, a Methodist minister. Helms collected used household goods and clothing in wealthier areas of the city, then trained and hired the poor and immigrants to mend and repair the used goods. The goods were then resold or were given to the people who repaired them. The system worked, and the Goodwill philosophy of "a hand up, not a hand out" was born.

Cheddar Cheese and Olive Balls

Anna C. Balzano
Goodwill Staff

2 cups shredded sharp Cheddar cheese, set until room temperature
½ cup butter or margarine, softened
½ teaspoon paprika
Pinch of dry mustard
Pinch of cayenne
¾ cup flour
40 small stuffed olives, well drained

Combine Cheddar cheese, butter, paprika, dry mustard, and cayenne in a large mixing bowl or food processor. Mix well. Add flour and mix until a smooth, well blended dough is formed. Cover and let stand in a warm, dry place for 20 minutes.

   Preheat oven to 375º. Divide dough into 40 equal pieces. Flatten each piece and place an olive in the center. Bring dough edges together to envelope olive. Roll gently between palms to form a ball. Place on an ungreased baking sheet. Bake for 20 minutes or until golden brown.

   Note: The recipe can be made ahead of time. Wrap balls well and freeze. Bake, unfrozen, for 30 minutes.

Serves 10
Complexity: Easy

About the Recipe
At a family gathering, it seems we always talk about food and exchange ideas. We wanted to try something different. It's all done by experimenting. Our sister-in-law came up with the measurements.

Scotch Eggs

Lamont M. Davis
Goodwill Staff

3 pounds sausage meat
4 teaspoons dried sage
Salt and pepper
Flour, enough to coat
4 eggs, beaten
Breadcrumbs, enough to coat
1 dozen hard-boiled eggs, peeled
Vegetable oil

Mix together sausage and dried sage. Season well with salt and pepper. Place flour, beaten eggs, and breadcrumbs in three separate bowls. Flour hands and roll a portion of sausage meat into a ball around each hard-boiled egg. Dip in beaten eggs and then in breadcrumbs.

Fill a large saucepan halfway with oil and heat until hot enough for frying (about 375º). Fry eggs in oil for 6 to 7 minutes. (Do be careful! Place only a few eggs in the oil at a time. The oil will boil and foam, so watch it constantly.) Remove eggs from oil and drain on paper towels.

Serve hot (as some restaurants do) or cold (much better!) with a salad. Scotch eggs will keep in the refrigerator for one week. They will not freeze well.

Serves 6
Complexity: Moderate

About the Recipe

My mother has served these as breakfast, lunch, and dinner. They also pack well for a picnic or camping trip.

Deviled Eggs

Ann McKamey
Receptionist, Graver Technology

12 eggs
2 tablespoons mayonnaise
1 tablespoon mustard
1 teaspoon red wine vinegar, optional
Paprika

Place eggs in a pan large enough to hold them without crowding and cover with cold water. Heat until water boils. Remove pan from heat, cover, and let stand (off heat) for 15 to 18 minutes.

Drain and run cold water in the pan. When eggs are cooled down, peel and cut in half lengthwise. Scoop out yolks and place in a mixing bowl. Mash eggs with a fork or place in a blender. Mix in mayonnaise, mustard, and vinegar. (Texture of yolk mixture should be smooth and solid, not runny.) When finished mixing, place yolk mixture inside eggs. Sprinkle each egg with paprika.

Note: The filling is the most important part of the recipe. Mayonnaise makes the texture of the filling softer and smoother. The more times you make these, the better they get. You'll find out you won't measure after a while because you'll know what the filling should taste, feel, and look like.

Serves 12 to 24
Complexity: Easy

About the Recipe

I was in my twenties when I learned this recipe. It was given to me by a good friend and neighbor when we lived on Lincoln Street in Wilmington. She was a great Italian cook! She taught me a lot. We stayed up many late nights when holidays were coming about. She still lives in the same house today and is still cooking!

Stuffed Mushrooms

Tara Shockley
Friend of Goodwill

1½ pounds crabmeat
4 cups breadcrumbs
2 eggs
1 green bell pepper, chopped
Salt
Pepper
Old Bay Seasoning
1 tablespoon butter
1 pound (12 to 16) large button mushrooms, stems removed
½ cup melted butter

Combine crabmeat, breadcrumbs, eggs, and green pepper in a large bowl. Season to taste with salt, pepper and Old Bay.

Preheat oven to 375º. Grease a baking pan with 1 tablespoon butter. Place mushrooms on pan. Stuff with crabmeat mixture. Pour melted butter over mushrooms. Bake for 20 minutes.

Serves 6 to 8
Complexity: Easy

About the Recipe

A seafood lover's treat that's a party and holiday favorite around our house.

Sausage Rounds

Kristin Strouss
Goodwill Staff

1 pound ground beef
1 pound bulk hot sausage
1 pound Velveeta cheese, cubed
1 tablespoon Worcestershire sauce
2 teaspoons Italian seasoning
1 teaspoon garlic salt
3 loaves party rye bread

Brown ground beef and sausage separately. Drain well and combine. Mix meats with remaining ingredients, except bread, and stir until cheese is melted. Spread mixture on bread. Place on cookie sheets and seal in plastic bags. Freeze until ready to use.
Preheat oven to 350º. Bake for 12 minutes. Serve hot.

Serves 15 to 20
Complexity: Moderate

About the Recipe
This is a make-ahead appetizer. You can also use pumpernickel party bread.

Bruschetta

Eric Orsetti

Chef, Valle Cucina Italiana Restaurant

12 cloves garlic, minced
1 to 2 large red tomatoes, sliced thin and then halved
6 ounces prosciutto ham, diced
1 cup olive oil
1 teaspoon crushed red pepper
1 teaspoon salt
1 teaspoon pepper
1 teaspoon garlic powder
½ bunch fresh parsley, minced
1 large loaf Italian bread
8 ounces mozzarella cheese, shredded

Preheat oven to 475°. Combine all ingredients except bread and mozzarella. Slice Italian bread on bias into about 12 pieces. Top bread slices with tomato mixture and spread evenly. Sprinkle with mozzarella cheese. Place on baking sheet and bake until golden brown. Remove and serve.

Serves 4 to 6
Complexity: Easy

About Goodwill

The organization, formally incorporated in 1910 and housed in Boston's Morgan Memorial Chapel, became known as Morgan Memorial Cooperative Industries and Stores, Inc. It provided job skills training programs and even a rudimentary placement service. The name "Goodwill Industries" was later adopted after a Brooklyn, NY, workshop coined the phrase.

Portobello a la Crème

Bob Older
President, Creative Travel/Goodwill Board Member

½ cup olive oil
1 clove garlic, peeled and minced
1 tablespoon balsamic vinegar
1 pound portobello mushrooms, cleaned and cut into ½-inch slices
2 tablespoons butter
2 tablespoons finely chopped shallots
Salt and pepper to taste
¾ cup heavy cream

Combine olive oil, garlic, and balsamic vinegar. Place mushrooms in a shallow bowl and cover with marinade. Marinate in the refrigerator for 4 to 6 hours.

Preheat broiler to 450º. Remove mushrooms from marinade and place on a baking sheet. Broil for 3 minutes or until tender. Reserve.

Melt butter in a small saucepan. Add shallots and sauté. Season with salt and pepper. Add cream and reduce until slightly thickened.

Place mushrooms on serving dishes and top with cream.

Serves 4
Complexity: Easy

About Goodwill
Coffee bags served as the first collection bags for "Morgan Chapel Industrial Relief Work." Thomas Wood & Company donated the first thousand burlap bags. Later, Chase & Sanborn Company donated many thousands of bags. [Photo from Morgan Memorial Goodwill Industries, Inc.]

Seafood Quesadilla

Bob Older

President, Creative Travel/Goodwill Board Member

½ cup white wine
¼ pound scallops, cut in half
¼ pound cooked crabmeat
¼ pound cooked small shrimp
½ cup milk
1 slice of onion
2 peppercorns
1 bay leaf
2 tablespoons flour
1 tablespoon butter
Salt and pepper to taste
8 large flour tortillas
⅛ cup heavy cream
4 tablespoons grated Gruyere cheese

Preheat oven to 400°. Heat a large skillet. Add wine and reduce by half. Add scallops, cook until white, about 2 to 3 minutes. Remove scallops with slotted spoon. Retain juice. Combine scallops, crabmeat, and shrimp together in a small bowl. Reserve.

Heat a medium-sized saucepan. Add milk, onion, peppercorns, and bay leaf and slowly bring to a boil, stirring constantly. Strain milk to remove solids. Place milk back in pan.

In a small bowl, combine 2 tablespoons of milk mixture with flour and whisk until smooth. Add flour mixture back to milk in pan. Add butter and salt and pepper and stir until thickened.

Add three-quarters of milk mixture to the seafood and mix well. Place 4 tortillas on baking sheets. Cover tortillas with seafood mixture and top with remaining tortillas. Reserve.

Preheat oven to 400°. Add leftover scallop juice to remaining milk and bring to a boil. Add cream and mix well. Spoon mixture over tortillas. Sprinkle each with cheese. Bake for 12 to 15 minutes or until tops are golden brown.

Serves 4
Complexity: Difficult

Exotic Mushrooms Angelucci

Mark Chew
Owner, Courtney's

2 tablespoons olive oil
½ pound oyster mushrooms, washed and sliced
½ pound shiitake mushrooms, washed and sliced
1 clove garlic, sliced
1 shallot, chopped
5 leaves fresh basil, minced
5 ounces Basic Marinara Sauce (Recipe appears on page 152.)
2 tablespoons chopped black olives
Pinch of salt and freshly ground pepper
1 tablespoon butter
Minced parsley

Heat olive oil in a large sauté pan. Sauté mushrooms, garlic, shallot, and basil for a few minutes.

Add marinara sauce to the pan along with olives and salt and pepper. Simmer, uncovered, until mushrooms are tender. Swirl in butter at the last minute to thicken the sauce. Taste and adjust seasonings. Garnish with parsley and serve hot accompanied by fresh bread.

Serves 2
Complexity: Easy

About Goodwill

An early collection wagon outside Boston's Morgan Memorial Chapel. Pictured at far right is Brother Thomas F. Benbury, an African-American minister and friend of Edgar J. Helms. [Photo from Morgan Memorial Goodwill Industries, Inc.]

Grilled Portobellos au Poivre

Mark Chew
Owner, Courtney's

Olive oil
1 pound portobello mushrooms, cleaned and stems removed
2 cups beef stock
1 tablespoon brandy
1 tablespoon freshly ground black pepper
Pinch of dried oregano
Pinch of salt
1 teaspoon flour
1 tablespoon unsalted butter
Minced fresh parsley

Coat sauté pan with olive oil. Add mushrooms and cook over medium heat until tender. Transfer to a plate and keep warm.

In same pan over high heat, combine stock, brandy, black pepper, oregano, and salt. Bring to a boil. Reduce heat.

Mix together flour and butter. Swirl mixture into the liquid and cook until sauce thickens. Pour sauce over mushrooms. Garnish with parsley. Serve immediately alone or with sliced fresh bread.

Serves 2
Complexity: Medium

About Goodwill

In 1919, Rev. John H. Beauchamp founded Goodwill Industries of Delaware & Delaware County. Incorporated in 1921, the Asbury M.E. Church in Wilmington, DE, was the first home of the organization. Insert Rev. Henry S. Dulaney, Pastor. [Circa 1902.]

Crab Custard and Spinach Mousse with Sweet Yellow Pepper Puree

Leo Medisch
Chef, Back Porch Cafe

2 9-ounce packages frozen leaf spinach
2 small onions, finely chopped
2 whole eggs
10 egg yolks
4 cups Lewes Dairy cream
1 pound jumbo lump crabmeat
Salt, white pepper, and nutmeg to taste
Sweet Yellow Pepper Puree (Recipe appears on page 154.)

Simmer spinach until it is bright green and just thawed. Do not overcook. Rinse with cold water. Pack into a 2-cup measuring cup, squeezing out excess water. (Yields 2 cups.)

Sauté onion until translucent. Combine half of cooked onion, spinach, 1 whole egg, 5 egg yolks, 2 cups cream, and seasonings in a food processor fitted with a metal blade. Process until well blended. Reserve.

In a large bowl, whisk togeher remaining whole egg, yolks, and cream until well blended. Add crabmeat, remaining cooked onion, and seasonings.

Preheat oven to 400º. Butter 6 six-ounce timbale molds (or ovenproof bowls) thoroughly. Fill molds halfway with crab mixture. Cover to the rim with spinach mousse. Knock mold on a table or counter to settle contents. Cover with buttered foil and bake in a water bath for 45 minutes or until a knife inserted in center comes out clean. Let rest for 10 minutes before serving.

Run a paring knife around the timbale mold and invert on to a plate. Cover with yellow pepper puree and serve immediately.

Serves 6
Complexity: Difficult

About the Recipe

This is an elegant and light first course offered at our restaurant, using backfin crabmeat, a local delicacy. A simple grilled veal chop or an herbed roast leg of lamb would be a perfect complement.

Sa

ads

Field Green Salad with Toasted Pumpkin Seed Vinaigrette

Neil R. Elsohn

Executive Chef/Owner, Waters Edge Restaurant

¼ cup pumpkin seeds, toasted
¼ cup rice wine vinegar
Juice of 1 lime
¾ cup extra virgin olive oil
Coarse salt and freshly cracked pepper to taste
6 cups field greens
6 ounces "Coach Farm" goat cheese
1½ cups chopped mixed tropical fruits (mango, papaya, star fruit, pineapple, or your
  choice)

Puree pumpkin seeds, vinegar, and lime juice in a processor. Slowly drizzle in olive oil.
Season to taste with salt and pepper. Toss vinaigrette with remaining ingredients. Eat!

Serves 4
Complexity: Easy

About Goodwill

People lined up each day to receive services from Goodwill Industries. [Circa 1933.]

Orange-Jicama Spinach Salad

Nancy Little

ESL Instructor, Del-Tech, New Castle County Vo Tech

4 oranges, peeled and sectioned (or 2 to 3 small cans mandarin oranges, drained)
1 pound jicama, peeled and cut into 2 x ¼-inch strips
1 medium-sized purple onion, thinly sliced
⅓ cup orange juice
⅓ cup olive oil
¼ cup lime juice
2 tablespoons red wine vinegar (or balsamic)
Salt and freshly ground pepper
8 cups torn raw spinach leaves (or romaine lettuce)
Toasted sliced almonds or pine nuts

Combine oranges, jicama, and onion rings in a large bowl. Toss and set aside.

Whisk together orange juice, olive oil, lime juice, and red wine vinegar. Season to taste with salt and fresh ground pepper. Add to orange mixture and gently toss. Cover and chill for at least 2 hours.

To serve, add spinach and nuts to orange mixture and toss well.

Serves 8
Complexity: Moderate

About the Recipe

This is three different salad recipes that I've combined into one. It's terrific for a party or large family gathering. Add grilled chicken or mild fish to make it into a main course. In the spring and early summer, I add sliced strawberries.

Summer Salad for One

Charles "Ebbie" Alfree III
Goodwill Staff

Handful of spinach or spring mix
8 to 10 cherry tomatoes
1 stalk celery, chopped
1 carrot, peeled and chopped
1 small can mandarin oranges
Handful of pecans or sliced almonds
1 package of roasted chicken strips (about 8 ounces)
Handful shredded white Cheddar cheese
Bottled raspberry vinaigrette dressing

Place spinach or spring mix in a large serving bowl. Add tomatoes, celery, and carrots. Add chicken, pecans or almonds, and mandarin oranges. Cover with cheese. Pour in as much dressing as you like. Mix and eat!

Serves 1 or 2
Complexity: Easy

About Goodwill

The early Goodwill Industries taught workers to refurbish and repair donations such as shoes.

Not-What-You'd-Expect Celery Salad

Amy Rand

Chief Brain, BrainCore, Inc./Goodwill Board Member

Bunch of celery
Blue cheese, crumbled
Olive oil
Fleur de sel (or kosher salt)

Wash celery thoroughly and slice crosswise into ½-inch pieces. Toss celery with blue cheese and enough olive oil to coat. Season with fleur de sel to taste. Serve immediately.

Serves 2
Complexity: Easy

About the Recipe

In Hong Kong, a single stalk of celery goes for about nine dollars. This is because celery is used in traditional Chinese medicine to treat high blood pressure. Western scientists use compounds from this lowly vegetable to develop new drugs to treat hypertension. This recipe is really yummy, and if we didn't think of celery as such a basic food, it would be served in the finest restaurants. As this is a very simple recipe, the finest ingredients give the best results. Eat it and be healthy!

Celery and Apple Salad Dijon

Lamont M. Davis
Goodwill Staff

4 tablespoons mayonnaise
2 tablespoons Dijon mustard
2 teaspoons cider vinegar
½ teaspoon sugar
½ teaspoon dried, crumbled tarragon leaves or parsley
Salt and pepper
8 ribs celery, cut into 1½-inch match sticks
2 Granny Smith apples, peeled and cut into 1½-inch match sticks

Whisk together mayonnaise, mustard, vinegar, sugar, and tarragon. Add salt and pepper to taste. Whisk until the dressing is smooth. Add the celery and apples. Toss and serve.

Serves 4
Complexity: Easy

About the Recipe

This is one of my favorite salads to have with barbecue. The ingredients are small and easy to transport, making it a nice addition to our campsite meals.

Blood Orange and Fennel Salad

Bob Older

President, Creative Travel/Goodwill Board Member

1 small bulb fennel
2 tablespoons lemon juice
2 tablespoons olive oil
1 tablespoon balsamic vinegar
2 tablespoons minced mint
Salt and pepper to taste
2 blood oranges, peeled and sliced into wheels

Cut tops off fennel and reserve. Wash bulb and slice into very thin strips.

Combine lemon juice, olive oil, balsamic oil, and mint in a mixing bowl. Season to taste with salt and pepper. Remove one-quarter of the dressing and reserve. Add fennel to remaining dressing and toss together. Let sit for 30 minutes.

Mound fennel on a plate. Ring with blood orange wheels. Drizzle reserved dressing over oranges and garnish with fennel tops.

Serves 2
Complexity: Easy

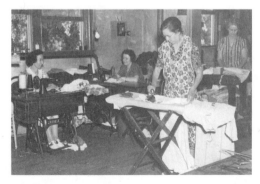

About Goodwill

Goodwill employees learned to mend and clean soiled clothing.

Broccoli Salad

Shirley Jester
Office Clerk

1 cup mayonnaise
½ cup sugar
2 tablespoons white vinegar
2 tablespoons cider vinegar
1 bunch broccoli, chopped small
1 pound bacon, cooked, cooled, and crumbled
1 red onion, chopped small
1 8-ounce package yellow shredded sharp Cheddar cheese

Combine mayonnaise, sugar, and vinegars. (For best results, make the sauce the day before.)

Combine broccoli, bacon, onion, and most of the cheese in a serving bowl. Pour sauce over mixture and mix well. Sprinkle with remaining cheese.

Serves 4
Complexity: Easy

About Goodwill

The doors of Morgan Memorial Goodwill Industries were always open — no matter what time of day, no matter what the need. [Photo from "The House of Goodwill," Morgan Memorial Press, 1925.]

Red Bliss Potato Crab Salad

Joe Brown
Chef/Owner, Melange Cafe

6 to 8 red bliss potatoes, skin on
½ cup chopped onion
1 to 2 teaspoons dried parsley
¼ cup red wine vinegar
¼ cup olive oil
½ cup warm chicken stock
1 teaspoon sugar
1 cup jumbo lump crabmeat, picked clean
Salt and pepper

Cook potatoes in boiling water until fork-tender, about 12 to 15 minutes. Strain and cool. Slice when cool enough to handle.

Combine remaining ingredients, except crabmeat and salt and pepper, in a bowl. Mix in potato slices. Gently fold in crabmeat and season with salt and pepper. Serve immediately or refrigerate and serve chilled.

Serves 4
Complexity: Easy

About the Recipe

This recipe is from "Joe Brown's Melange Cafe Cookbook" which features 100 of the most popular and requested recipes from Melange Cafe in Cherry Hill, NJ. Crabmeat adds a little twist to the traditional German potato salad. Although this is a perfect side dish for any picnic, try serving it as a casual main course, adding romaine lettuce and slices of Jersey tomato and avocado.

Asian Slaw

Tom Hannum
Executive Chef, The Hotel duPont

¼ pound snow peas, cleaned and finely julienned
½ red pepper, finely julienned
2 shiitake mushrooms, finely sliced
½ medium carrot, finely julienned
2 ounces snow pea shoots
1 medium red onion, thinly sliced
4 tablespoons rice wine vinegar
½ cup plus 2 tablespoons vegetable oil
2 tablespoons sesame oil
Salt and white pepper

Place vegetables in a bowl. In a separate bowl, whisk together vinegar and oils. Toss vegetables with enough vinaigrette to coat. Season to taste with salt and pepper.

Serves 4
Complexity: Easy

About Goodwill

Children had a special place in the heart of Goodwill founder Edgar J. Helms. Even in its earliest days, Goodwill was strengthening families. [Photo from Morgan Memorial Goodwill Industries, Inc.]

Mediterranean Cole Slaw

Jon Hallowell
Executive Chef/Owner, Mixmaster Café

1 head cabbage
1 large carrot
1 red onion
2 teaspoons dry basil
2 teaspoons dry oregano
½ cup honey
½ cup extra virgin olive oil
¼ cup red wine vinegar
4 cloves garlic, minced
Salt and pepper

Shred cabbage, carrot, and onion to desired consistency and place in a large bowl. Combine remaining ingredients, add to bowl, and toss well. Season with salt and pepper to taste.

Serves 8
Complexity: Easy

About the Recipe

Because it has no mayonnaise, this recipe is a healthy alternative to traditional cole slaw. It keeps well for picnics and outdoor summer fun and is a nice side dish for sandwiches.

Sou

MILWAUKEE EDITION

VOL. 2. MARCH, APRIL, MAY, 1921 No. 3.

THE GOODWILL

GOODWILL INDUST.

INDEPENDENCE

CHARACTER

TRAINING

WORK

SHELTER

FOOD

NOT CHARITY, BUT A CHANCE!

ups

Quick Mushroom Soup

Mark Chew
Owner, Courtney's

½ pound unsalted butter
1 onion, diced
3 pounds white mushrooms, de-stemmed, washed, and diced
3 tablespoons beef stock
Pinch of salt
Pinch of freshly ground pepper
Pinch of dried oregano
2 quarts heavy cream
Roux of flour and butter

Heat butter in a large pot. Sauté onions until translucent. Add mushrooms and beef stock; cook together for 3 minutes. Add salt, pepper, oregano, and heavy cream. Simmer until mushrooms are tender.

Before serving, heat soup and thicken with roux. Adjust seasonings. Serve hot.

Serves 4 to 6
Complexity: Easy

About Goodwill
Unloading donations at Goodwill Industries.

Cream of Broccoli Soup

Gerry Treese
Chef Instructor, Food Bank of Delaware

3 medium russet potatoes, peeled and diced to ⅜ inch
½ pound butter
3 cloves garlic
1 yellow onion, diced to ¼ inch
1 rib celery, sliced
½ pound carrots, sliced
1 bunch broccoli, stems and florets separated
7 ounces flour (about 1 cup)
1 quart milk, scalded
2 quarts chicken stock
4 ounces Cheddar or Monterey cheese, optional
¼ teaspoon EACH thyme, white pepper, salt

Cover potatoes with cold water and bring to a boil. Simmer until slightly soft. Remove from heat and reserve. (Do not drain; water needed.)

Melt butter in a large saucepan. Add garlic and onion and sauté until clear (do not brown). Slice broccoli stems into thin strips. Add stems, celery, and carrots to pan. Cook for 8 to 10 minutes over low flame. Add flour and cook slowly for 2 to 3 minutes. Add potatoes and water, milk, chicken stock, and cheese. Adjust consistency with more milk, if desired. Add thyme, pepper, and salt.

Blanch broccoli florets and then cool down with ice. Add florets just before serving.

Serves 6 to 8
Complexity: Moderate

About the Recipe

Other vegetables – carrot, mushroom, etc. – can be substituted for broccoli. Great with hot bread or salad.

Pumpkin Soup

Dale Wolf
Former Governor of Delaware

2 cups peeled, diced pumpkin or butternut squash
4 cups chicken broth
1 whole nutmeg, grated
1-inch piece peeled fresh ginger root
½ teaspoon salt
1½ cups heavy cream

Place pumpkin, chicken broth, nutmeg, ginger, and salt in a saucepan. Cover and simmer until pumpkin is tender and mushy, about 15 to 20 minutes. Press mixture through a sieve or puree in a food mill, blender, or processor. Return to saucepan. Stir in 1 cup cream and reheat until hot.

Whip remaining cream. Serve with whipped cream and additional grated nutmeg on top.

Serves 4
Complexity: Easy

About Goodwill
Goodwill Industries' employee who suffered from rheumatoid arthritis begins her day at work.

Curried Squash and Pear Soup

Cathy McCartan

Print Consultant, Modern Press Inc.

2¼ pounds butternut squash
2 tablespoons butter
1½ cups chopped onion
3 medium to large pears, peeled, cored, and diced
1½ teaspoons curry powder
1½ teaspoons paprika
4 to 4½ cups low-sodium chicken broth
⅓ cup half-and-half
Salt and fresh ground pepper to taste

Cut squash in half, remove seeds and place in a pan with 1 inch of water. Cover and cook over low heat until fork tender, but not mushy (20 to 30 minutes). (Squash can also be microwaved. Cut in half and put in a microwavable container, cover with plastic wrap, and microwave on high until tender, about 6 minutes.) When cool, peel and cut squash into chunks.

Melt butter in a saucepan. Add onion and sauté until tender, about 5 minutes. Add squash chunks, pear pieces, curry powder, and paprika; sauté 5 minutes longer. Add 4 cups chicken broth and cook covered at a light simmer until squash and pears are very tender, about 15 minutes.

Puree in a blender. Add remaining broth or more if needed. Add half-and-half and salt and pepper to taste. Heat through. Do not boil.

Serves 6
Complexity: Moderate

About the Recipe

This recipe requires time to peel and dice the ingredients. If I have pears that are overripe, I peel and dice them, add a little lemon juice, and freeze them until I am ready to make the soup. This soup also freezes well. Just omit half-and-half and add when ready to serve.

Clam Chowder

Dale Wolf

Former Governor of Delaware

3 pieces bacon, chopped coarse
1 cup onions, chopped fine
2¼ cups peeled and cubed potatoes
1 cup water
1 bay leaf
Pinch of cayenne
1 10½-ounce can whole baby clams with liquid
½ cup clam liquid
½ pint half-and-half
2 tablespoons butter
½ cup sherry
Salt to taste
White pepper to taste
Black pepper to taste

In a soup pot, sauté bacon until almost crisp. Remove bacon from pan and reserve. In same pan, sauté onions in bacon drippings. Add bacon, potatoes, water, bay leaf, and cayenne. Cook until tender.

Add clams, clam liquid, half-and-half, and butter. Cook until thick. Do NOT boil. Season with sherry, salt, white pepper, and black pepper.

Serves 4
Complexity: Easy

About Goodwill

Since the incorporation of Goodwill Industries, the revenue generated through Goodwill's businesses has supported the Goodwill mission. [Circa 1951.]

Shrimp Bisque

Beverley Brainard Fleming

Data Analyst, Astrazeneca

2 pounds raw shrimp, peeled and chopped
¼ cup chopped mushrooms
2 tablespoons chopped onion
2 tablespoons chopped celery
1 tablespoon chopped carrot
3 tablespoons melted butter
Salt to taste
Cayenne pepper to taste
2 cups chicken broth
1½ cups light cream
½ cup dry white wine

Sauté shrimp and vegetables in melted butter over low heat for about 2 minutes. Stir in salt, cayenne, and chicken broth. Bring to a boil and cook for 20 minutes. Pour shrimp mixture into an electric blender; blend until smooth. Combine shrimp puree, light cream, and wine in a saucepan. Heat thoroughly. Serve immediately.

Serves 6
Complexity: Easy

About the Recipe

Use shrimp or lobster. Either way this is a tasty treat for those cold winter nights or a special dinner party.

Not-Just-Any-Chili Chili

Judy Hurd

Executive Assistant, Food Bank of Delaware

2 pounds lean ground beef (or turkey)
1 large onion, coarsely chopped
1 28-ounce can tomatoes
1 15-ounce can tomato puree
1 can kidney beans, drained
1 can chili beans
1 12-ounce can beer (or 1½ cups water)
3 tablespoons Worcestershire sauce
3 cloves garlic, minced or pressed
1 beef bouillon cube
1 tablespoon chili powder
1 teaspoon crushed red pepper
1 teaspoon EACH ground coriander, ground cumin, thyme, oregano, and basil
2 bay leaves
Shredded Cheddar cheese
Sour cream
Sliced green onions (including tops)

Crumble beef or turkey into a 5- to 6-quart kettle over medium heat. Cook, stirring to break up, until browned. Add onion and cook until soft. Stir in tomatoes (break up with a spoon) and liquid, tomato puree, beans, beer, Worcestershire, garlic, bouillon cube, chili powder, red pepper, coriander, cumin, thyme, oregano, basil, and bay leaves.

Bring to a boil; reduce heat and simmer, uncovered, stirring occasionally, until chili is thick and flavors are well blended (about 2 hours). Skim, discard fat, and remove bay leaves.

Pour into bowls and pass cheese, sour cream, and onions to spoon over individual servings.

Serves 6 to 8
Complexity: Easy

About the Recipe
I won local (Lancaster, PA) Chili Cook-off Contest in 1995 with this recipe, which was handed down from my mother.

Sweet Spicy Chili

Tara Shockley
Friend of Goodwill

2 large jars Prego tomato sauce
1 cup honey
1 medium-size jalapeño pepper, chopped
1 pound hamburger or ground chicken
2 large green bell peppers, chopped
1 large onion, chopped
Salt
Pepper
Old Bay Seasoning
3 15.5-ounce cans kidney beans
Cooked rice

Heat sauce, honey, and jalapeño pepper in a large stockpot. Simmer. Meanwhile, fry meat, bell peppers, and onion in a skillet until meat is brown. Add spices to taste. Add meat mixture and beans to sauce and let simmer for 45 minutes. Stir occasionally. Serve over rice.

Serves 5 to 7
Complexity: Moderate

About the Recipe
Another experiment recipe from the Shockley kitchen gone good!!

Outer Banks Gazpacho

Ted Van Name
Goodwill Staff

2 large ripe tomatoes, peeled and chopped
1 large red pepper, peeled and chopped
1 clove garlic, minced
1 sweet onion, peeled and minced
1 cucumber, peeled and chopped
24 ounces V-8 Juice
2 tablespoons olive oil
2 tablespoons red vinegar
2 tablespoons lemon juice
½ teaspoon Worcestershire sauce
½ cup mixed chopped herbs - chives, parsley, basil, chervil, tarragon
Salt and pepper to taste
Tabasco sauce to taste

If you are patient, you can finely chop all the vegetables or you can place not so finely chopped vegetables in a blender for 2 or 3 minutes.

Place all ingredients in a glass bowl, cover tightly, and refrigerate for at least 4 hours.

Serves 6
Complexity: Moderate

About the Recipe

This recipe "traveled" to the Outer Banks, NC, for many summer vacations. Usually on the 2nd day while you need a break from the beach, we'd put on some good tunes and start chopping and blending. The soup hits its peak on the 4th or 5th day and was surely gone before the trip home.

Peach Buttermilk Soup

Cathy McCartan
Print Consultant, Modern Press Inc.

2 pounds ripe peaches
1 cup buttermilk
1 cup light cream or nonfat evaporated milk
⅓ cup orange juice concentrate
⅛ teaspoon cinnamon
⅛ teaspoon cloves
⅛ teaspoon allspice

Drop peaches into boiling water for no longer than count of 10. Peel under cold running water and remove pits. Puree in blender and pour into medium bowl and add remaining ingredients. Stir to blend well.

Place soup in refrigerator for 6 hours or overnight. If desired, garnish with toasted coconut or toasted slivered almonds.

Serves 6 to 8
Complexity: Easy

About Goodwill

One of the many important jobs at a Goodwill store was to attach price tags to merchandise. Here a Goodwill employee learns to operate a pricing machine. [Circa 1950.]

Ent

ees

Rice Stuffed Chicken Breast
with Dijon Cream Sauce

Tim Rawlins

Chef, Valle Cucina Italiana Restaurant

½ cup mushrooms
¼ cup diced roasted peppers
1 shallot, diced
2 cups cooked rice (cooked until tender)
4 boneless chicken breast halves (4 to 6 ounces each), pounded
2 cups flour
3 eggs, beaten
4 cups breadcrumbs
2 tablespoons olive oil
Toothpicks
Dijon Cream Sauce (Recipe appears on page 152.)

Combine mushrooms, peppers, and shallot in a sauté pan and sauté until mushrooms are tender. Fold in rice and set aside.

Preheat oven to 350º. Place pounded chicken breasts on work surface. Place rice mixture in the center of each breast. Roll chicken to cover mixture and secure with toothpicks. Dredge each rolled chicken breast first in flour, then beaten eggs, then breadcrumbs.

Heat oil in a large ovenproof skillet. Add chicken and brown. Transfer pan to oven and bake until chicken is cooked through, about 25 to 30 minutes.

Arrange baked chicken breast on platter and drizzle with Dijon cream sauce.

Serves 4
Complexity: Moderate

About the Recipe
I like to serve this to my family at Christmas.

Easy Chicken and Rice Casserole

Kristin Strouss
Goodwill Staff

1 box Uncle Ben's Wild and Long Grain Rice
1 chicken, cut into 8 serving pieces (or 8 boneless chicken breast halves, about 4 to 6
   ounces each)
1 can cream of mushroom soup
1 can cream of celery soup
1½ cans water

Preheat oven to 350°. Grease bottom of 9 x 12-inch baking dish. Pour rice on bottom
of dish. Arrange chicken on top of rice. Mix together soups, water, and seasoning
from rice and pour over top of chicken. Bake uncovered for 1½ to 2 hours. (You can
cover with foil after 1 hour, if getting too brown.)

Serves 6
Complexity: Easy

About Goodwill

*To better serve the community, Goodwill began partnering with other
not-for-profit organizations such as the Boy Scouts. [Circa 1955.]*

Chicken Casserole

Kristen Tosh

Music Teacher, George Read Middle School

1 box chicken–flavor stuffing
1 16-ounce bag frozen broccoli spears or florets, defrosted enough to separate
1 pound cooked chicken, cut into 1-inch cubes
8 ounces Velveeta Cheese, cubed
½ cup milk
Small can French fried onions

Preheat oven to 350º. Prepare the stuffing without cooking. (Use cold water and mix well.) Spread the stuffing in the bottom of a casserole dish. Spread broccoli pieces in a single layer over the stuffing. Spread the chicken in a single layer over the broccoli.

Place the cheese cubes in a microwave-safe dish. Add milk. Microwave, stirring often, until it becomes a creamy cheese sauce. Pour the cheese sauce over the chicken.

Cover the casserole dish with foil or a lid and bake for about 45 minutes.

Uncover and sprinkle the onions generously on top. Continue baking, uncovered, for another 15 minutes or until the onions are golden brown.

Serves 6
Complexity: Easy

About the Recipe

This recipe can be doubled for large gatherings and prepared the night before for a hassle-free family day!

Sticky Chicken

Rebecca Castro
Friend of Goodwill

1 whole chicken, cut into 8 serving pieces
2½ to 3 cups granulated sugar
Hot water (enough to cover chicken)
1 small bottle soy sauce

Arrange chicken pieces in a single layer in a large cast-iron skillet. Cover chicken with sugar until completely coated. Add enough hot water to fill pan and cover chicken. Add soy sauce to make water in pan appear black (about ¾ bottle). Cook on high heat, turning often, until liquid is completely caramelized. Serve immediately with a side dish of steamed vegetables. Bon appetit!

Serves 4 to 5
Complexity: Moderate

About the Recipe

I used to experiment with different recipes at slumber parties when I was younger. This has been a favorite of my friends ever since. (We won't go into how many years ago now!)

Caribbean Curry Chicken

Dorothy W. Webb
Retired

1 cup water
¼ cup rum
1½ teaspoons garlic powder
1½ teaspoons curry powder
1 cube chicken bouillon
½ pound fresh mushrooms, sliced or 1 3-ounce can mushrooms, drained
2 chicken breasts, split and skinned or 4 chicken thighs, skinned
2 to 3 teaspoons cornstarch

In a large skillet, combine water, rum, garlic and curry powders, and bouillon cube and bring to a boil. Add mushrooms, reduce heat, and simmer for 5 to 10 minutes. Add chicken, cover, and simmer for 25 to 30 minutes or until tender.

Blend cornstarch with 2 tablespoons water and slowly stir into pan until sauce thickens. Place chicken on a warm platter and pour sauce over chicken.

Serves 4
Complexity: Easy

About the Recipe
This is good served over rice, even mash potatoes! Serve extra gravy in a bowl. Apple juice may be substituted for rum.

Grilled Caribbean Chicken

Kristen Tosh

Music Teacher, George Read Middle School

2 boneless chicken breasts, pounded
Olive oil or Pam spray
Emeril's "Bam!" spices to taste
1 15.2-ounce can Dole Tropical Fruit Mix
¼ teaspoon chili pepper paste
1 bag washed salad greens (Milano style is best.)

Preheat the grill. Spray chicken breasts with olive oil and season with spices to taste. Grill chicken, about 7 minutes each side, until juices run clear and the middle shows white.

As the chicken cooks you can prepare the topping. Drain about half the juice from the can of fruit. Pour remaining juice and fruit into a plastic bowl. Stir in chili pepper paste. Mix well.

Place a bed of salad on each plate. When the chicken is ready, place directly on the salad and top with the fruit mixture.

Serves 2
Complexity: Easy

About Goodwill

Goodwill employee prepares paychecks on a graphotype machine.

Lime Chicken

Patrick Little

President, Little Industries, Inc./Past Goodwill Board Member

¼ cup fresh lime juice
2 tablespoons sherry
2 tablespoons olive oil
½ teaspoon oregano
½ teaspoon garlic powder or 1 to 2 cloves garlic, finely chopped
Salt
4 skinless boneless chicken breast halves

Mix together lime juice, sherry, olive oil, oregano, garlic, and salt to taste in a non-reactive dish or bowl. Add chicken breasts and turn to coat thoroughly. Marinate in refrigerator for 1 hour.

Remove chicken from marinade. Put marinade into a small saucepan and boil for at least 1 minute.

Preheat grill. Grill chicken breasts, brushing with boiled marinade, until fork tender, about 4 to 6 minutes per side. Serve with softened tortillas and salsa.

Serves 4
Complexity: Easy

About the Recipe

This recipe is slightly adapted from one that won the Delmarva Chicken Cooking Contest some years ago. I make this on a regular basis, and it can easily be doubled.

Chicken Cacciatore

Anna C. Balzano
Goodwill Staff

2½ to 3 pounds broiler-fryer chicken, cut into 8 serving pieces
¼ cup olive oil
2 medium onions, cut into ¼-inch slices
1 16-ounce can plum tomatoes, peeled
1 8-ounce can seasoned tomato sauce
2 cloves garlic, minced
½ teaspoon salt
¼ teaspoon pepper
½ teaspoon celery seed
½ teaspoon crushed oregano
2 bay leaves

Brown chicken pieces slowly in oil over medium heat. Remove from skillet. Cook onions in same oil until tender, but not brown. Add remaining ingredients and mix.

Return chicken to pan, cover, and simmer for 45 minutes. Turn chicken occasionally and be careful not to boil. Uncover and cook about 15 minutes longer or until chicken is tender and sauce is the consistency of chili sauce.

Skim off excess fat and remove bay leaves before serving.

Serves 6
Complexity: Moderate

About the Recipe

When I married into an Italian family, my mother-in-law hand wrote all meals for me to prepare for her son. She herself was taught by her mother who was originally from Italy.

Splattered Chicken Pasta

William C. Mackrides

Attorney and Counselor at Law/Goodwill Board Member

Olive oil
1 large onion, minced
4 large chicken breasts, cut into bite-size pieces
1 large chicken breast, cooked and well shredded
5 cloves garlic or 1 teaspoon garlic powder
½ cup water
1 tablespoon soy sauce
1 teaspoon parsley
½ teaspoon cayenne pepper or garlic chili sauce
½ teaspoon salt
Black pepper
½ cup breadcrumbs
Bourbon to taste, optional
1 pound cooked linguine
Grated sharp provolone cheese
Chopped scallions
Sour cream, optional

Heat oil in a large sauté pan. Sauté onion until translucent. Add chicken pieces and cook a few minutes. Add shredded chicken, garlic, water, seasonings, breadcrumbs, and bourbon and cook until heated through and thickened slightly. Pour over hot linguine. Serve topped with provolone, chopped scallions, and sour cream.

Serves 4 to 8
Complexity: Moderate

About Goodwill

Originally a faith-based organization, employees attended church services at the Goodwill Industries' chapel. [December 24, 1958.]

Cape Fillet of Beef

Brian Parker

Executive Chef, The Southern Mansion Bed & Breakfast

Butter or olive oil
4 8-ounce beef tenderloins
12 shiitake mushrooms
2 teaspoons minced garlic
10 strands fresh thyme
8 sage leaves
2 sprigs rosemary
1 teaspoon black pepper
4 tablespoons red balsamic vinegar
4 tablespoons Merlot wine
Beef stock (canned is fine)
1 cup demi-glace (available in most supermarkets or gourmet stores)

Heat a large sauté pan over medium-high heat. Add enough butter or oil to coat pan. Add beef and brown on each side.

Add mushrooms, garlic, and herbs. Add vinegar and wine. If liquid dries too quickly, add a little beef stock. Cook until desired doneness.

Remove herbs. Stir in demi-glace. Serve beef covered in sauce.

Serves 4
Complexity: Moderate

About Goodwill

The cycle of donations, processing, resale, and wages was the beginning of Goodwill Industries — and essentially remained intact over the past century.

Becca's Blue Ribbon Meat Loaf

Rebecca Castro
Friend of Goodwill

2 pounds ground beef
1 pound ground sausage
2 green onions, diced
½ cup grated Cheddar cheese
1 bell pepper, finely chopped
1 packet onion soup mix
1 packet mushroom soup mix
3 eggs
1 cup crushed barbecue chips
Salt, pepper, and garlic salt to taste
Italian seasonings to taste
1 tablespoon EACH soy sauce, Worcestershire sauce, Louisiana hot sauce
1 tablespoon plus ¼ cup A-1 Steak Sauce
1 small can tomato sauce
1 can tomato paste
Parsley flakes

Preheat oven to 350°. Combine all ingredients, except ¼ cup A-1 Sauce, tomato paste, and parsley flakes, until evenly mixed. Place into a large loaf pan and bake for 3 hours, draining excess fat as needed during cooking.

Remove meat loaf from oven. Mix together ¼ cup A-1 Sauce and tomato paste and pour over meat loaf. Sprinkle with parsley flakes. Return to oven and bake another 30 minutes. Slice and serve warm.

Serves 4 to 8
Complexity: Easy

About the Recipe

Becca won a blue ribbon with this recipe — her first main course country fair entry. She was just 13. Her Home Economics teacher convinced her to enter. It works great with mashed potatoes and sweet butter corn as side dishes with a side salad.

Calico Beans

Patricia D. Beebe
President/CEO, Food Bank of Delaware

6 slices bacon
1 medium onion, chopped
½ pound ground chuck
¾ cup brown sugar
½ cup catsup
1 teaspoon salt
1 teaspoon dry mustard
2 teaspoons vinegar
1 16-ounce can pork and beans
1 16-ounce can kidney, chick, black, or pinto beans, partially drained
1 16-ounce can lima or butter beans, partially drained

Fry bacon until crisp. Crumble and reserve.
  Preheat oven to 350°. Sauté onion in the bacon fat. Add beef. Combine cooked beef and onion, brown sugar, catsup, salt, dry mustard, vinegar, pork and beans, and selected beans and place in a 3-quart baking dish. Sprinkle with bacon. Bake for 40 minutes.

Serves 4 to 6
Complexity: Moderate

About the Recipe
A family favorite for picnics, this recipe came from my mother's metal recipe box from my Aunt Helen in Baton Rouge, Louisiana.

Taco Toss

Rebecca Castro
Friend of Goodwill

2 pounds ground beef, cooked
2 packages taco seasoning mix
2 pounds sharp Cheddar cheese, grated
2 9-ounce bags nacho flavored Doritos, crushed
2 large tomatoes, diced
1 head iceberg lettuce, chopped
1 bunch green onions, diced
Salt, pepper, and garlic salt to taste
1 pint sour cream
1 small bottle picante sauce

Mix ground beef and taco seasoning together until well blended. Add ¼ cup water to moisten, if needed. Mix in all remaining ingredients except sour cream and picante sauce. Serve in cereal bowls. Top with sour cream and picante sauce.

Serves 6 to 10
Complexity: Easy

About the Recipe

A light and easy-to-make meal. This recipe is a tradition for the Castro family for New Year's and all quick holiday parties.

Jerk Roasted Pork Tenderloin

Damian Durnin

Chef de Cuisine, Columbus Inn

2 cloves garlic
2 shallots, peeled and chopped
1 ounce pineapple juice
Juice of 1 small lime
1 tablespoon dark rum
1 tablespoon red wine vinegar
1 tablespoon dark brown sugar
1 teaspoon peeled and chopped fresh ginger
1 teaspoon fresh thyme
1 teaspoon ground nutmeg
1 teaspoon ground allspice
1 teaspoon ground cinnamon
Pinch of crushed red pepper
Salt and pepper to taste
2 pork tenderloins, about 2 pounds total

Combine all ingredients, except pork, in a food processor and puree. Transfer to a saucepan and simmer for 5 minutes. Cool and refrigerate. Coat pork with marinade about 2 to 4 hours before cooking.

Cook on the grill or in a 400° oven or pan sear over medium heat. Cook for about 15 minutes or until medium (160°). Slice to serve.

Serves 4
Complexity: Easy

About the Recipe

This dish is one of the most versatile ever. Ask the Jamaicans! Pork tenderloin usually comes tightly packaged from any good butcher and more often than not on the meat shelf in your local supermarket. Any combination of starch and vegetables can be used as a main course or simply place atop your favorite salad for a lighter meal or appetizer. (Fish, chicken, turkey, or even beef can be substituted for the pork.)

Pot Roast Pork

Pete Kledaras
Friend of Goodwill

3 pounds boneless pork loin
Salt and pepper
3 tablespoons fennel seeds
3 tablespoons butter
Olive oil
½ bottle Chardonnay
8 cloves garlic, skins on
4 bay leaves
1 fennel bulb, sliced
Handful of fresh rosemary

Roll up pork loin and tie tight with butcher's twine. Season with salt and pepper and cover with fennel seeds.

Preheat oven to 400°. Heat oil and half the butter in a roaster pan over medium-high heat. Add loin and fry until golden. Add remaining ingredients. Remove from stove top and insert a meat thermometer. Cover loosely and transfer to oven. Roast until internal temperature is 150° to 160°. (It will cook fast.)

Serves 6
Complexity: Easy

About the Recipe

While touring France with my wife, we got lost. A kind bed and breakfast owner invited us to stay and have this wonderful dinner. So on the rest of the trip we got lost often.

Deer Hash

Tara Shockley
Friend of Goodwill

1 pound ground deer meat
Cooking oil
Salt and pepper to taste
6 large potatoes, peeled and diced
1 large onion, chopped
1 large bell pepper, chopped
1 clove garlic, chopped
Butter

Brown deer in a little oil in a large skillet until light brown. Season with salt and pepper and reserve.

In a separate pan, sauté potatoes, onion, bell pepper, and garlic in butter until soft. Add mixture to deer meat and stir to combine. Cook unil heated through.

Serves 4
Complexity: Easy

About the Recipe

This recipe came about out of boredom. I wanted something different to eat and decided to experiment. The family loved it so I kept making it.

Honey-Teriyaki Glazed Salmon with Asian Slaw

Tom Hannum
Executive Chef, The Hotel duPont

¼ cup honey
½ cup teriyaki sauce
1 tablespoon Worcestershire sauce
2 tablespoons plus 1 teaspoon packed brown sugar
1 tablespoon sesame oil
¼ cup orange juice
1 clove garlic, chopped
1 tablespoon chopped fresh ginger
2 scallions, finely chopped
4 5-ounce salmon fillets
Cooking oil
Asian Slaw (Recipe appears on page 36.)

Combine first 9 ingredients in a bowl and mix well. Place enough marinade over salmon to coat well and let stand for 15 to 30 minutes. Place remaining marinade in a saucepan and cook until liquid is reduced by half. Strain and reserve.

Preheat sauté pan over medium-high heat. Add a few tablespoons of cooking oil. Add salmon pieces and sauté approximately 5 to 7 minutes depending on thickness of fish and desired doneness.

Serve with Asian slaw and drizzle with reduced marinade.

Serves 4
Complexity: Easy

About the Recipe
I made this recipe when I was featured on the CBS Saturday morning show "The Early Show" on a segment called Chef on a Shoestring. This recipe can be an appetizer or entree, served cold, warm, or hot.

Rice Paper-Roast Asian Salmon

Albert Paris

Executive Chef, Zanzibar Blue

4 12-inch rice paper wrappers
4 Thai bird chiles (Jalapeño or Serrano peppers can be substituted.)
1 bunch fresh cilantro, stems removed
8 jumbo shrimp, peeled and deveined
12 jumbo scallops
4 6-ounce pieces boneless skinless salmon
2 teaspoons kosher salt
2 teaspoons black cracked pepper
2 tablespoons peanut oil

Preheat oven to 425º. Dip the rice paper wrappers in warm water and place on a damp towel. Top each wrapper with 1 bird chili and then with cilantro leaves. Place 2 shrimp on the right side of the cilantro and 3 scallops on the left. Top with 1 salmon fillet. Season with salt and pepper. Roll like a package and spread with oil.

Roast, pepper side up, on a sheet pan for 12 minutes until rice paper is golden and translucent. Serve with a scallion shi/taki broth (available in Asian stores) and a slice of lime.

Serves 4
Complexity: Moderate

About the Recipe

Delving into the Martial Arts over the last seven years has afforded me some wonderful experiences. One aspect of the training is taking the sifu *(teacher) out to dine, enjoying what is known as Kung Fu life: sharing experiences and searching for the meaning, purpose, and intentions in one's life. In one of these 3 a.m. sessions, I found myself in a lovely Vietnamese restaurant in Philadelphia's Chinatown, dining on clayroast salmon and shrimp and Vietnamese spring rolls wrapped in the silken and unusual texture of fresh, unfried rice paper. As with all new dishes, this inspiration came from the separating and reintroducing of these ingredients in a new way. This is the dish that came to pass.*

Whole Roasted Black Bass in Sea Salt Crust

James Barnes
Owner, The Dilworthtown Inn

1 pound coarse crystal sea salt
1 bunch rosemary
1 bunch thyme
4 cups all-purpose flour
2 cups egg whites
1½ pounds black sea bass, gutted, scaled, and fins trimmed
1 lemon
2 cloves garlic
Egg wash
Extra virgin olive oil
Preserved lemon peel

Mix sea salt and herbs in the bowl of a food processor. Chop for 2 minutes. Transfer mixture to a mixing bowl with a dough hook attachment. Add flour and mix. Continue mixing and slowly add the egg whites until the dough forms a ball. Place dough on a sheet tray, wrap in plastic, and refrigerate overnight.

Remove the dough 30 minutes before prep time. Roll out to ¼-inch and cut dough in half. Line a tray with parchment paper and lay out half of the dough. Place fish on dough and stuff fish with lemon and garlic. Spread egg wash around the fish and cover with the rest of the dough. Spread egg wash on top and sprinkle with a little more sea salt. Refrigerate for 30 minutes before baking.

Preheat a convection oven to 375º. Bake for 20 minutes. Let rest for 5 minutes and then cut around the crust. (Do not eat the crust.) Serve with olive oil and preserved lemon.

Serves 4
Complexity: Difficult

About Goodwill

A goodwill employee, who suffered from infantile paralysis, repairs a fan.

Chilean Sea Bass Special

Joe Moro
Chef, Ristorante La Locanda

4 tablespoons honey
1 tablespoon balsamic vinegar
1 pound Chilean sea bass fillet, cut into 4 pieces
Salt and pepper
5 ounces graham cracker crumbs
½ cup vegetable oil

Combine honey and balsamic vinegar and reserve.

Season fish with salt and pepper to taste. Place graham cracker crumbs in a shallow bowl. Dredge fish in crumbs and cover completely. Heat oil in a frying pan until very hot. Carefully place fish in pan. Cook for about 1 or 2 minutes per side, depending on thickness and desired doneness.

Place 2 pieces of fish on each plate. Drizzle with honey dressing. Serve with the vegetable of your choice.

Serves 2
Complexity: Moderate

About Goodwill

All people, regardless of their background, race, or creed, were welcomed at Goodwill Industries.

Fish Veracruz

Dorothy W. Webb
Retired

¼ cup oil
2 cups diced onions
1 14.5-ounce can diced tomatoes, drained, juice reserved
1½ tablespoons minced garlic
1 cup small pimento stuffed olives
¼ cup capers, drained and lightly rinsed
1 teaspoon dried oregano
1 teaspoon crushed parsley flakes
2½ to 3 pounds white fish, cut into fillets (snapper, bass, mahi mahi, etc.)
1 small lemon

Heat oil in a large skillet over medium heat. Sauté onions until soft, about 5 minutes. Add garlic and sauté another minute. Add tomatoes and break up the tomatoes a little. Add remaining ingredients, except fish and lemon. Bring to a boil. Reduce heat and simmer uncovered for 25 minutes. Stir occasionally. If necessary, add some of the reserved juice to sauce.

Preheat oven to 350°. Arrange fish in an 11 x 14 x 2-inch baking dish. Squeeze juice from lemon over fish and top with sauce. Bake uncovered for 55 minutes. (Yes, 55 minutes is right. Fish will remain flaky.)

Serves 4 to 6
Complexity: Moderate

About the Recipe

This is best served over rice. A couple dashes of hot sauce can be added to the sauce for a little extra zing. Two cans of diced tomatoes can be used for more sauce, if desired.

Grandpop Ruoff's Crab Cakes

Diane McGonagle
Office Manager

4 tablespoons butter
4 tablespoons shortening
¾ cup flour
1 cup milk
2 teaspoons Worcestershire sauce
½ teaspoon dry mustard
1 teaspoon salt
Pinch of mace
1 medium onion, finely chopped
1 pound crabmeat, fresh or canned
Breadcrumbs

Combine butter, shortening, flour, milk, Worcestershire sauce, and dry mustard in a saucepan and cook on medium heat until sauce thickens. Add onion and simmer for 15 minutes, being careful not to let sauce brown. Remove from pan and cool, then carefully stir in crabmeat. Refrigerate overnight.

When ready to cook, shape cold mixture into 1-inch-thick patties. Roll in fine breadcrumbs.

Place enough shortening or oil in a heavy pot to cover crab cakes. Heat over medium-high heat until hot (about 350º). Carefully lower crab cakes into hot fat and fry until golden brown. Drain and serve.

Serves 4
Complexity: Moderate

About the Recipe

This is my grandfather's recipe. He and my five uncles would go crabbing all day and then come back and make these wonderful cakes for us ... fond memories of the seashore in the '50s.

Shrimp and Crab Mousse Cakes

Tom Hannum

Executive Chef, The Hotel duPont

1 pound shrimp, peeled and deveined
2 eggs
½ quart heavy cream
Salt and white pepper to taste
3 to 4 dashes Worcestershire sauce
2 to 3 dashes Tabasco sauce
1½ bunches scallions, greens only, chopped and sautéed
1 pound jumbo lump crabmeat, picked clean
1 to 2 tablespoons Dijon mustard
Clarified butter or vegetable oil
Champagne Mustard Sauce (Recipe appears on page 153.)

Mince shrimp in a food processor. Add eggs and blend well. Add heavy cream and blend to make a mousse. Transfer to a stainless steel bowl. Add next 6 ingredients.

Heat a nonstick pan over medium heat. Add clarified butter or vegetable oil. Use an ice cream scoop to form cakes and drop cakes directly into the pan. Brown on both sides. (Can be finished in a hot oven if cakes are thick.) Serve with champagne mustard sauce.

Serves 6
Complexity: Moderate

About the Recipe

This can be served as an hors d'oeuvre, appetizer, or entree, depending on size portion used.

Shrimp Scampi

Janet Doto
Goodwill Staff

1½ tablespoons olive oil
12 jumbo shrimp, peeled and deveined
Salt and pepper to taste
1 tablespoon minced garlic
⅓ cup dry white wine
Juice from 1 lemon
2 plum tomatoes, finely chopped
1 tablespoon chopped fresh dill or 1 teaspoon dried dill
6 tablespoons butter, cut into small pieces

Heat oil in a large pan over medium-high heat until hot. Season shrimp with salt and pepper. Sauté shrimp for 2 to 3 minutes on each side. Remove shrimp from pan and pour out all but a little oil. Add garlic and sauté for about 1 minute. Add wine and lemon juice and cook until liquid is reduced by half. Add tomatoes and cook for 2 minutes. Reduce heat to medium-low.

    Add butter, a little at a time, and cook until just melted. Add dill and shrimp and stir until well combined and heated through. Season to taste with salt and pepper. Serve over angel hair or capellini pasta.

Serves 4 or 5
Complexity: Moderate

About Goodwill
Use of booths and bins for collection of donations was a major development for Goodwill in the 1960s. [Newark Shopping Center, Newark, DE.]

Spicy Shrimp

Colleen Morrone
Goodwill Staff

½ cup olive oil
2 tablespoons Cajun seasoning
2 tablespoons lemon juice
2 tablespoons fresh parsley or cilantro
1 tablespoon honey
1 tablespoon soy sauce
Cayenne pepper to taste
1 pound shrimp, peeled and deveined
1 pound cooked linguine

Place all ingredients, except pasta, in a casserole dish and mix until well blended. Cover and refrigerate for 1 hour.

Preheat oven to 450º. Cook for 10 minutes or until shrimp are fully cooked. Serve over hot pasta.

Serves 4
Complexity: Easy

About the Recipe

A favorite recipe from our friend Rich Przywara. Leftovers are terrific in omelets the next day.

Vieux Carré Scampi

Arline Docherty
Goodwill Staff

1½ pounds shrimp
2 tablespoons lemon juice
½ teaspoon lemon-pepper marinade (available in stores)
½ teaspoon salt
1 green onion, finely chopped
4 sprigs parsley, chopped
¼ teaspoon mace
Pinch of garlic powder
3 tablespoons butter, thinly sliced
2 ounces Long Horn cheese, thinly sliced

Preheat oven to 350º. Place shrimp in a buttered baking dish. Cover with lemon juice. Sprinkle with lemon-pepper marinade and salt. Combine green onions, parsley, mace, and garlic powder and sprinkle over shrimp. Top with butter and cheese.

Bake for 15 to 20 minutes. Serve immediately with rice, tossed green salad, and French bread. (Shrimp can be reheated in a regular or microwave oven.)

Serves 4
Complexity: Easy

About the Recipe

This was the first meal I made for my husband before we were married. He thought I was a great cook. Little did he know that at the time, this was the only meal I could make!

Eggplant Parmesan

Cathy Kipp
Goodwill Staff

1 large eggplant
3 large eggs
1 cup breadcrumbs
1 teaspoon onion powder
½ cup olive oil
16 ounces tomato sauce
2 tablespoons oregano
2 tablespoons Parmesan cheese
1 pound mozzarella cheese, shredded

Peel entire eggplant and remove stem at top. Slice eggplant into ½-inch pieces. Whisk eggs in a small bowl. Mix breadcrumbs and onion powder together on a plate.

Place olive oil into a frying pan and set at medium heat. Dip each eggplant slice into the eggs and then bread on both sides with breadcrumb mixture. Place in hot frying pan and fry until both sides are golden brown. (You may have to fry several batches but continue to use same oil.)

Place a single layer of fried eggplant slices on the bottom of a large casserole dish. Place a thin layer of tomato sauce over eggplant. Sprinkle with oregano and Parmesan to taste. Place a thin layer of mozzarella cheese over sauce. Repeat with a layer of eggplant, sauce, seasonings, and mozzarella. Continue layering until all eggplant slices are used.

Cover dish with plastic wrap and microwave for 8 minutes at a power level of 70%.

Serves 3 to 4
Complexity: Moderate

About the Recipe
This recipe has been in my family for over 20 years and is served for almost every holiday. Best served with any type of pasta.

Mushrooms Fra Diavolo

Mark Chew
Owner, Courtney's

1 tablespoon olive oil
2 cloves garlic, sliced
½ pound shiitake mushrooms, sliced
½ pound oyster mushrooms, sliced
5 leaves fresh basil, torn
1 jalapeño pepper, roasted with seeds left in
5 ounces marinara sauce
Pinch of dried oregano
Pinch of freshly ground pepper
1 tablespoon butter
Minced parsley

Heat oil in a large frying pan. Sauté garlic until brown. Add the mushrooms, basil, jalapeño pepper, marinara sauce, and seasonings. Cook until mushrooms are tender. Swirl in butter at the end of cooking. Garnish with parsley and serve.

Serves 2
Complexity: Easy

About Goodwill
A woman operates a switchboard using a Braille board as her guide dog lends his support. [Photo from Goodwill Industries of America News, March 13, 1972.]

Vidalia Onion Pie

Doug Cornforth
Goodwill Board Member

1 cup Ritz cracker crumbs
½ stick butter, melted
2 cups sliced Vidalia onions
2 tablespoons butter
2 eggs
¾ cup milk
¾ teaspoon salt
Dash of pepper
¼ cup grated sharp Cheddar cheese
Paprika
Parsley

Preheat oven to 350°. Mix Ritz crumbs and melted butter. Press into an 8-inch pie plate. Sauté onions with 2 tablespoons butter until clear, not brown. Spoon into pie crust. Beat eggs with milk, salt, and pepper and pour over onions. Sprinkle on cheese and paprika. Bake for 30 minutes. Sprinkle with parsley before serving.

Serves 6
Complexity: Moderate

About the Recipe

Recipe from Ann Wynn, Wynn Farms, Vidalia, Georgia.

Vegetarian Shepherd's Pie

Lara M. Zeises
Author, BRINGING UP THE BONES (Delacorte 2002)

2 large sweet potatoes
2 tablespoons margarine
½ cup plain soy milk
Salt and pepper to taste
1 tablespoon olive oil
½ medium onion, chopped
2 cloves garlic, minced
1 12-ounce bag Morningstar Farms burger crumbles
1 16.5-ounce can vegetarian mushroom gravy
Your favorite seasonings (basil, oregano, etc.) to taste
1 12-ounce can mixed peas and carrots, drained
1 12-ounce can corn, drained

Preheat oven to 350°. Peel sweet potatoes and cut into medium-size chunks. Boil for 20 minutes or until tender. Drain and mash with margarine and soy milk. Add salt and pepper and set aside.

In a large frying pan, heat olive oil and sweat onions and garlic until translucent. Add frozen burger crumbles and stir to soak up oil and juices. After 3 to 5 minutes, add mushroom gravy and stir until well combined. Add your favorite seasonings and mix well. Turn off heat.

In a 9 x 9-inch casserole dish, spread heated crumbles mixture. Top with canned vegetables, then spread mashed potato mixture on top, making sure it reaches edges of pan. Bake for 40 minutes. Serve hot.

Serves 4
Complexity: Easy

About the Recipe

One of my favorite childhood dishes was my mother's Shepherd's Pie. It was always so warm and comforting during the winter. But when I gave up eating meat, I had to find vegetarian alternatives to my favorite dishes. This version is easy to make; and I've served it to at least one confirmed steak eater who not only asked for seconds, but wanted the recipe as well.

Pas

NOT CHARITY, BUT A CHANCE!

tas

Pasta with Four Cheeses

Cathy McCartan

Print Consultant, Modern Press Inc.

¼ cup unsalted butter
¼ cup flour
1½ cups milk
1 28- to 32-ounce can whole Italian tomatoes, chopped
Salt and pepper to taste
1 pound bow tie pasta
6 ounces mozzarella cheese, grated
2 ounces Gorgonzola, crumbled
2 ounces Italian fontina cheese, diced
1 cup fresh grated Romano cheese
½ cup chopped flat-leaf parsley

Preheat oven to 375°. Melt butter in a saucepan. Add flour and whisk for about 3 minutes to form a roux. Add milk and bring to a boil, whisking. Stir in tomatoes and salt and pepper to taste and simmer until thickened, about 3 minutes.

Meanwhile, cook pasta al dente and drain. Stir together sauce, pasta, and remaining ingredients. Pour into a 3- to 4-quart gratin dish. Bake for 30 to 35 minutes until bubbly.

Serves 6
Complexity: Easy

About Goodwill

Recycling is a priority for Goodwill Industries. The textile donations that do not meet Goodwill's quality criteria for retail sales are baled and sold to bale dealers. [Employee is operating a bale machine.]

Cheese Ravioli
with Gorgonzola Fig Cream

Jonathan Yanek
Chef, Columbus Inn

1 pound fresh cheese ravioli
1 medium sweet onion, julienned
1 tablespoon oil
¼ cup sherry
¼ cup chicken stock
½ pound Gorgonzola cheese
8 figs, quartered
Salt and pepper to taste

Cook ravioli until al dente. Drain and reserve.

Sauté onions in oil until caramelized. Add sherry and cook until liquid is reduced by half. Add chicken stock and cook until liquid is reduced by half. Slowly mix in Gorgonzola cheese. Fold in figs. Season with salt and pepper to taste.

Serves 4
Complexity: Moderate

About the Recipe
Very simple! I have cooked this for the family ... even the kids love it.

Homemade Gnocchi

Judi Pennella and Becky Masseth
Friends of Goodwill

1 cup ricotta cheese
2 cups flour
1 beaten egg

Mix together all ingredients, adding more ricotta if necessary so the ball of dough feels firm. (You may mix it in a bowl or in a food processor.) Knead the dough on a slightly floured board. Pull off a handful and roll it into a thin snake-like strip about the thickness of your little finger. Cut the strip into pieces, the size about the width of your thumb.

Shape the pieces by placing your thumb on a piece of dough and pushing and dragging the dough away from you while rotating your thumb on its side. If you do it correctly, the dough should curl and look sort of like a shell. You should end up with about 80 gnocchi.

Spread the shaped dough on a lint-free towel or a lightly floured cookie sheet to rest. They will dry slightly.

Boil a large pot of water. Gently drop the gnocchi into the water and boil for about 15 minutes, stirring occasionally. The gnocchi will rise to the top. Drain thoroughly. Serve with your favorite spaghetti sauce.

Serves 4
Complexity: Difficult

About Goodwill

Goodwill's full service commercial cleaning agency, Facility Maintenance Services, provides general cleaning, all surface floor care, outside ground and parking lot cleaning, and construction/ renovation cleanup.

Pregnancy Pasta

Amy Rand

Chief Brain, BrainCore, Inc./Goodwill Board Member

Box or bag of pasta
Olive oil
Package of frozen spinach or fresh spinach
Container of ricotta cheese
Nutmeg
Salt and pepper

Add pasta and a splash of olive oil to a large pot of boiling salted water and cook as directed on package. Meanwhile, thaw spinach in microwave, let it cool enough to touch, and then squeeze out all the moisture you can. (If using fresh spinach, poke a few holes in the bag and microwave for 2 minutes.)

Empty cooked pasta into a colander, reserving about 1 cup of cooking water. Transfer pasta back to pot. Stir in more olive oil so that the noodles are slippery. Add the ricotta, spinach, and a few shakes of nutmeg. Salt and pepper to taste. If the pasta is too sticky, add some of the reserved cooking water.

Serves one starving pregnant woman plus spouse
Complexity: Easy

About the Recipe

This is a very easy, very healthy way to get the phytonutrients and calcium needed during pregnancy. If you're bored with broccoli, try this. People who don't like spinach often like this recipe.

Exotic Mushrooms alla Bartolli

Mark Chew
Owner, Courtney's

2 tablespoons olive oil
½ pound oyster mushrooms, cleaned and sliced
½ pound shiitake mushrooms, cleaned and sliced
1 clove garlic, minced
¼ cup Marsala wine
Pinch of salt
Pinch of freshly ground pepper
Pinch of dried oregano
½ pound angel hair pasta
1 tablespoon blue cheese
1 tablespoon butter
Minced fresh parsley

Heat oil in a large heavy skillet. Sauté mushrooms and garlic over high heat. Lower the heat and add wine, salt, pepper, and oregano. Simmer until mushrooms are tender.

Meanwhile, cook the pasta until al dente. Drain and keep warm.

When ready to serve, add blue cheese and butter to the skillet. Cook for a few minutes until sauce thickens. Taste and adjust seasonings.

Pour mushrooms over pasta and toss. Garnish with parsley and serve immediately.

Serves 2
Complexity: Easy

About Goodwill

Goodwill's Contract Services provides companies with a cost-effective alternative to out sourcing labor-intensive production and time-consuming jobs.

Macaroni and Cheese

Jim Zeigler
Goodwill Staff

1 pound elbow macaroni or mini penne pasta
4 8-ounce cans tomato sauce
1½ pounds New York extra sharp Cheddar cheese, cut into ⅛-inch slices

Boil elbow macaroni for 8 minutes and drain thoroughly.

Preheat oven to 350°. Cover the bottom of a 10 x 10 x 3-inch baking dish with half the tomato sauce. Layer half the pasta over sauce. Cover with half the cheese. Repeat with another layer of sauce, macaroni, and cheese.

Bake for 45 minutes. Remove from oven and let stand for 5 minutes before serving.

Serves 4
Complexity: Easy

About the Recipe
This is an old recipe from my father's mother. I serve it with Italian bread or garlic bread and salad.

Side I

ishes

Asparagus Cashew Rice Pilaf

Kathi Birkofer
Registered Nurse/Stay-at-Home Mom

2 tablespoons butter
2 ounces uncooked spaghetti, broken
¼ cup minced onion
1 teaspoon minced garlic
1¼ cups uncooked jasmine rice
2¼ cups chicken broth
Salt and pepper to taste
½ pound fresh asparagus, trimmed and cut into 2-inch pieces
½ cup toasted cashew halves

Melt butter in a medium saucepan over medium-low heat. Increase heat to medium and stir in spaghetti, cooking until coated with the melted butter and lightly browned. Add onion and garlic and cook for about 2 minutes until tender. Stir in jasmine rice and cook for about 5 minutes. Pour in chicken broth. Season mixture with salt and pepper.

Bring the mixture to a boil. Reduce heat, cover, and simmer for 20 minutes until rice is tender and liquid has been absorbed.

Meanwhile, place asparagus in a separate medium saucepan with enough water to cover. Bring to a boil and cook until tender but firm. Drain.

Mix asparagus and cashew halves into the rice mixture and serve warm.

Serves 8
Complexity: Easy

About the Recipe
I originally got this recipe from www.allrecipes.com and have modified it slightly. I make it often for my family and for company. You can substitute vegetable broth for chicken and almonds for cashews.

Wild Rice

Tom Hannum
Executive Chef, The Hotel duPont

2 cups steamed wild rice
3 tablespoons honey
¼ cup diced dried fruits
¼ cup diced walnuts
Cracked black pepper

Preheat oven to 350°. Combine cooked rice, honey, dried fruits, and walnuts. Season with pepper to taste. Place in timbale molds and bake approximately 30 minutes in a water bath. Carefully unmold onto serving plates when ready to serve.

Serves 6
Complexity: Moderate

About Goodwill

Goodwill Staffing Services provides businesses with work-ready personnel. Skilled temporary employees are ready to fill clerical, secretarial, accounting, reception, data entry, warehouse, food service, and light industrial positions.

Smokey Mountain Rice

Allison Matthews
Art Teacher/Soccer Coach

4½ cups water
1 teaspoon salt
2 cups long grain rice
½ pound button or wild mushrooms, chopped
1 onion, chopped
4 slices bacon, cut into small pieces
Salt and pepper to taste

Bring salted water to a rolling boil in a lidded saucepan. Add rice, mushrooms, onion, and bacon. Reduce heat to low. Cover and cook for 20 minutes. Do not stir. Remove from heat and leave covered until serving time. Fluff with a fork just before serving. Season with salt and pepper to taste.

Serves 4
Complexity: Easy

About the Recipe

We thought up this recipe on a long car ride through the Smokey Mountains. It's easy and good and, like its name, has a smokey flavor.

Couscous Marrakesh

Bob Older

President, Creative Travel/Goodwill Board Member

⅓ cup butter

¾ cup chicken stock (to make vegetarian, use a mixture of wine and water)

¾ tablespoon salt and pepper

½ teaspoon saffron

½ teaspoon ground turmeric

1 small yellow onion, chopped

½ cinnamon stick

2 medium, very ripe tomatoes, peeled, seeded, and quartered

½ pound carrots, blanched and cut into 1-inch lengths

½ pound turnips, blanched and cut into ½-inch pieces

½ pound zucchini, cut into small pieces

½ pound cabbage, diced

⅓ cup chopped hot peppers

2 cups cooked couscous

Heat a large saucepan. Add all ingredients except cooked couscous. Cook on medium heat until tender, about 15 to 20 minutes.

To serve, place couscous in the center of plate and spoon mixture over couscous.

Serves 6
Complexity: Moderate

About Goodwill

Goodwill Industries' Computer Recycling Center opened in Newark, DE, in 1997. The Center, which repairs and sells donated computers, later moved to its current home at the Goodwill Center in Wilmington, DE.

Potato Casserole

Nan Hawkins
Innkeeper, Barnard Good House

4 cups peeled and shredded potatoes
¼ cup water
½ cup milk
3 tablespoons butter
2 eggs
1½ teaspoons salt
Pepper to taste
1 medium onion, diced
Paprika to taste

Preheat oven to 375º. Butter a medium casserole dish.

Place shredded potatoes in water to keep from discoloring. Set aside. Place water, milk, and butter in a saucepan. Cook over medium heat until just under boiling. Set aside.

Beat together eggs, salt, and pepper. Slowly add milk mixture to eggs, beating continuously. Mix well.

Drain potatoes well in a colander. Combine potatoes, onion, and egg mixture. Spoon mixture into prepared dish. Sprinkle with paprika. Bake uncovered for 50 minutes until edges are crusty.

Serves 6
Complexity: Easy

About Goodwill

Goodwill stores give people practical, real-world retail experience and prepares them for careers in the burgeoning retail industry.

Rosemary Ranch Potatoes

Christine Terranova
Stay-at-Home Mom

5 pounds red bliss potatoes, peeled and cubed
1 8-ounce package cream cheese, softened
1 1-ounce package ranch dressing mix
4 tablespoons heavy cream
Handful chopped fresh rosemary
Pinch of salt
Fresh cracked pepper

Bring a pot of salted water to a boil. Add potatoes and cook until tender but still firm. Drain and transfer to a large bowl.

Add cream cheese, dressing mix, cream, rosemary, salt, and pepper. Beat with a mixer until smooth. Serve immediately.

Serves 8
Complexity: Easy

About the Recipe

Every New Year's Eve we serve a midnight supper. These potatoes are always on the table in one form or another. Sometimes I marinate the potatoes in the ranch mix and rosemary, roast them, and then toss them with cream cheese.

Medley of Vegetables

Diane McGonagle
Office Manager

1½ cups carrots, cut into 2-inch long sticks
2 cups celery, cut into 2-inch long sticks
1½ cups sliced onions
4 tablespoons butter
3 tablespoons instant tapioca
1 tablespoon sugar (or more if desired)
2½ teaspoons salt
⅛ teaspoon pepper
2 cups diced canned tomatoes

Preheat oven to 350°. Cook carrots in boiling water for a few minutes. Drain carrots. Mix carrots and remaining ingredients together. Place in a 2-quart casserole dish and cover tightly. Bake for 1½ hours.

Serves 4
Complexity: Easy

About the Recipe
I have used this recipe for 25 years as an alternative to everyday veggies. You can use any fresh vegetables in this dish. In addition to the ones listed in the recipe, I have used zucchini, peppers, and potatoes. Gives vegetables some zest! Also good to double or triple for dinner parties.

Fennel Gratinée

Wendy K. Voss
Attorney, Potter Anderson & Corroon LLP/Goodwill Board Member

2 to 3 bulbs fresh fennel
1 tomato, diced
¼ to ½ cup fresh breadcrumbs
¼ cup grated Parmesan cheese
Olive oil

Clean, trim, and slice fennel into bite-size pieces. Blanch in lightly boiling water until just tender, approximately 4 to 5 minutes. Drain.

Preheat oven to 325°. Mix fennel and tomato in a buttered baking dish. Mix breadcrumbs and cheese and spread over fennel. Sprinkle with olive oil. Bake until heated through and breadcrumbs are slightly brown, approximately 20 to 30 minutes. May be prepared in advance.

Serves 4 to 6
Complexity: Easy

About the Recipe

This recipe makes a great and unusual Thanksgiving side dish. I devised it years ago while living in Austria at a time when much of the usual American Thanksgiving fare was not available, but the open-air markets were plentiful. For variety, substitute cauliflower for fennel.

Aunt Fanny's Squash Recipe

Dale Wolf

Former Governor of Delaware

3 pounds yellow squash
½ cup chopped onions
2 eggs
1 tablespoon sugar
1 teaspoon salt
½ teaspoon pepper
1 stick butter
½ cup breadcrumbs

Wash and cut squash. Boil until tender. Drain thoroughly.

Preheat oven to 375°. Mash together squash, onion, eggs, sugar, salt, and pepper.

Melt butter. Put squash mixture into a baking dish. Cover with melted butter. Sprinkle with breadcrumbs. Bake for 1 hour.

Serves 6
Complexity: Moderate

About Goodwill

Besides selling donations at Goodwill stores and at their General Auction, Goodwill Industries of Delaware & Delaware County is 1 of 86 Goodwill Industries registered to sell collectibles, fine china and jewelry, and designer clothing on Goodwill Industries' Internet auction site — shopgoodwill.com.

Brussels Sprouts
with Maple Mustard Sauce

Charlotte Ann Albertson

Owner, Charlotte-Ann Albertson's Cooking School

4 cups Brussels sprouts, trimmed
1 tablespoon sugar
2 tablespoons champagne vinegar
2 tablespoons balsamic vinegar
2 tablespoons maple syrup
2 tablespoons Dijon mustard
1 tablespoon coarse grain mustard
½ teaspoon salt
½ fresh ground pepper
⅛ teaspoon nutmeg
½ cup extra virgin olive oil

Make a cut in the base of each Brussels sprout and the bitter leaves will fall away. Cut an "X" in the bottom of each sprout. Bring 7 to 8 quarts water to a rapid boil. Add Brussels sprouts and sugar. When water returns to a boil, reduce heat and simmer for 5 to 8 minutes. Cool sprouts in a cold water bath and drain.

Whisk together remaining ingredients, except oil. Slowly add oil in a steady stream, whisking until mixture thickens. Toss sprouts with sauce and serve at room temperature.

Serves 4 to 6
Complexity: Moderate

About the Recipe
James Sherman was the owner and chef of Jamey's in Manayunk. He was also a popular teacher at Charlotte-Ann Albertson's Cooking School, and although he has since closed his restaurant and moved to Oregon, we still fondly remember him when we make this wonderful winter dish.

Caribbean Carrots

Dorothy W. Webb
Retired

1 16-ounce package frozen whole baby carrots
Rind from a small orange
8 tablespoons rum
4 ounces margarine
5 tablespoons brown sugar

Boil carrots in water with orange rind until done.

Meanwhile, carefully cook rum, margarine, and sugar in a large skillet, blending until clear. Drain carrots. Remove and discard rind. Add carrots to rum mixture. Stir gently to coat. Remove from heat and let sit at least 15 minutes. Reheat and serve.

Serves 4 to 6
Complexity: Easy

About the Recipe

Sprinkle with parsley flakes for a pretty look. Orange juice or apple juice can be substituted for the rum.

Nana's Cranberry Mold

The Cleaver Family
Friends of Goodwill

1 small package orange gelatin
1 cup hot water
1 large can whole cranberry sauce
1½ cups chopped walnuts
1 large naval orange, cut up in blender

Dissolve gelatin in hot water. Add whole cranberry sauce and mix well. Add nuts and orange and mix well. Spray a mold pan with nonstick spray. Spoon mixture into pan. Refrigerate overnight.
    Unmold onto plate lined with lettuce. Enjoy!

Note: This recipe can be made a few days ahead.

Serves 6 to 8
Complexity: Easy

About the Recipe
Every Thanksgiving the entire family would gather for a festive holiday, and we could always count on Nana's Cranberry Mold to be at the table. We have many memories of holidays and picnics with Nana and Pop Pop when this colorful mold would be placed on the table. We are happy to share this recipe with Goodwill Industries.

Dess

serts

Philadelphia German Butter Cake

Jeanette Kwiatkowski
Goodwill Staff

¼ cup granulated sugar
¼ cup shortening
¼ teaspoon salt
1 large egg
1 envelope active dry yeast
½ cup warm milk
2½ cups all-purpose flour
1 tablespoon vanilla

Butter Cake Topping
½ pound (2 sticks) unsalted butter (NO SUBSTITUTES)
⅔ cup flour
2 cups EXTRA FINE sugar
2 extra large eggs
4 to 5 tablespoons milk

Prepare dough by mixing sugar with shortening and salt. Add egg and beat with mixer for 1 minute until well blended. Dissolve yeast in warm milk. Add flour, then milk-yeast mixture and vanilla to dough batter. Mix 3 minutes with dough hook or by hand. Turn dough onto floured board; knead 1 minute. Place in a lightly greased bowl, cover with a towel, and set in a warm place to rise for 1 hour or until doubled.

To make topping, cream butter. In a separate bowl, stir together flour and sugar. Gradually beat sugar mixture into butter. Add eggs, one at a time, beating well after each addition. By the teaspoonful, add just enough milk to bring mixture to a consistency for easy spreading over cake, being careful not to make it too runny.

Divide dough in half. Roll or pat to fit two well-greased 8-inch square pans. (One 9 x 13 x 2-inch pan can be used in place of the two square pans.) Crimp edges half-way up sides of pans to hold topping in. When dough is spread, prick dough with a fork to prevent bubbling. Divide topping; spread over dough. Let cake stand for 20 minutes. Preheat oven to 375°.

Bake for 30 minutes or until done. Do not overbake. Topping should be crusty, but gooey. Let cool before cutting.

Serves 8 to 12
Complexity: Moderate

Mrs. Habbersett's Orange Almond Buttercake

Anita M. Cleaver

Administrative Manager, Creative Financial Concepts, Inc./Goodwill Board Member

1½ cups sugar
2 cups unsifted flour
1 tablespoon baking powder
½ teaspoon mace
½ pound butter, at room temperature
½ cup orange juice, at room temperature
4 eggs, at room temperature
1 teaspoon almond extract
2 tablespoons orange zest
1 tablespoon cornstarch
⅓ cup sugar
⅓ cup orange juice
Confectioners' sugar

Do NOT preheat oven. Cut out wax paper to fit bottom of a tube pan. Spray pan with nonstick spray.

Mix together sugar, flour, baking powder, and mace. Add butter, juice, eggs, and almond flavoring. Beat on high for 10 minutes, scraping sides of bowl often. After mixing, fold in orange zest. Pour into prepared tube pan and place on middle rack in COLD oven. Set temperature to 350° and bake for 50 minutes.

Fifteen minutes before cake is done, prepare orange glaze. Combine cornstarch and sugar in a small saucepan. Stir in orange juice until slightly thickened. Cook over medium heat. When cake is done, use a knife or large tined fork to open spaces in cake and pour in hot orange glaze. After 15 minutes, cut around pan and inside tube to loosen cake. Shake carefully until entirely free. Turn out on rack, right side up, and dust with confectioner's sugar. Dust again when cake is cooled.

Serves 6 to 10
Complexity: Moderate

About the Recipe

Thank you, Mrs. Habbersett, for this wonderful recipe! For a delicious pound cake variation, substitute milk for orange juice and eliminate zest and glaze. Frost with chocolate frosting.

Grandma's Pound Cake

Alice Smith
Friend of Goodwill

3 sticks butter
3 cups sifted sugar
5 eggs
3 cups sifted cake flour
1 cup whole milk
1 teaspoon baking powder
1 teaspoon salt
1 teaspoon vanilla extract
1 teaspoon lemon extract

Preheat oven to 350º. Grease a Bundt cake pan. Coat with flour and shake off excess.

Cream butter and sugar. Add one egg and a little flour. Then add another egg and a little milk. Add the rest of the eggs, flour, milk, baking powder, and salt. Add vanilla and lemon extracts. Beat until smooth, about 5 minutes. Pour into prepared pan and bake for about 75 minutes. Let cool.

Serves 10
Complexity: Easy

About the Recipe

This is my grandmother's recipe. She received it from her great-grandmother. My great-grandmother died at the age of 95. I was 11 years old.

Fruit Cocktail Cake

Marie Capiccotti
Friend of Goodwill

2 eggs
½ cup Crisco oil
1½ cups sugar
2 cups flour
2 teaspoons baking soda
½ teaspoon salt
1 28-ounce can fruit cocktail in syrup
Shaved coconut
1 can vanilla icing

Preheat oven to 350º. Grease a Bundt cake pan.

Mix together first 7 ingredients (including fruit cocktail syrup). Pour cake batter into prepared pan. Sprinkle coconut on top of batter. Bake for 45 minutes. Let cake cool and then ice.

Serves 5 to 10
Complexity: Easy

About the Recipe

This was my aunt's recipe. Every Sunday I would visit her, and she would always make a different cake for dessert; but this was my favorite.

Carrot Cake

Mark Weischedel
Past Goodwill Board Member

2 cups flour
2 cups sugar
2 teaspoons baking powder
2 teaspoons baking soda
1 teaspoon salt
3 teaspoons cinnamon
1¼ cups canola oil
1 pound carrots, peeled and grated
4 extra large eggs
½ cup chopped nuts
½ cup raisins or chopped pineapple, optional
2 teaspoons vanilla extract
¼ cup finely chopped carrots, optional
Cream Cheese Frosting (Recipe appears on page 111.)

Preheat oven to 350º. Grease and flour two 8-inch round cake pans.

Combine flour, sugar, baking powder, soda, salt, and cinnamon in a large mixing bowl. Mix with beater until well blended, about 3 to 4 minutes. Add oil and blend. Add grated carrots and eggs, one at a time, mixing well after each addition. Stir in nuts, raisins or pineapple, and vanilla and mix well.

Divide batter evenly between cake pans. Bake for 45 to 55 minutes or until cake springs back when lightly touched. Cool in pans for 5 to 10 minutes, then remove and cool completely on racks.

Frost cakes. Sprinkle chopped carrots over frosting as decoration, if desired.

Serves 8 to 12
Complexity: Easy

Variation: To make a sheet cake, follow cake recipe, using a 9 x 13-inch rectangular pan. Increase baking time by 5 minutes. If there is any extra frosting, it freezes well and can be used for the next time, or as a nice topping on cinnamon buns.

About Goodwill
Selling automobiles at a reasonable price, Goodwill Industries operates Delaware's only not-for-profit auto auction.

Cream Cheese Frosting

Mark Weischedel
Past Goodwill Board Member

8 ounces cream cheese, softened (regular or light, not fat free)
½ cup butter, softened
1 pound confectioners' sugar

Combine cream cheese and butter in a medium mixing bowl and beat until fluffy. Add sugar and beat to blend. (Use more or less sugar to reach desired consistency.)

About the Recipe

This recipe is from my mother-in-law, Judy Hannan. It's a family favorite that appears regularly around birthdays, holidays, and other family occasions. We tell ourselves that the carrots qualify it as a health food. If she uses light cream cheese, I'll have two slices! The optional raisins or pineapple and crunchy chopped carrots add a nice flavor and texture contrast. Feel free to experiment with other dried fruits as substitutes for the raisins.

Chocolate Peanut Butter Pie

Mickey Burns

Registered Nurse, New Castle County Government

1½ cups chocolate wafer cookie crumbs
3 tablespoons plus 1 cup sugar
5 tablespoons unsalted butter, melted
8 ounces cream cheese
1 cup creamy peanut butter (I like Skippy.)
2 cups chilled heavy cream
1 cup semi-sweet chocolate chips

Preheat oven to 350º. Blend crumbs, 3 tablespoons sugar, and butter in a bowl. Press crumb mixture into bottom and sides of a 9-inch pie plate. Bake in middle of oven for 10 minutes. Let cool.

Beat cream cheese and peanut butter in a large bowl until smooth. Beat remaining sugar into peanut butter mixture until well combined. Set aside. Whip 1½ cups heavy cream in a chilled bowl until it forms soft peaks. Fold one-quarter of whipped cream into peanut butter mixture. Fold in remaining whipped cream gently, but thoroughly. Mound mixture into prepared crust. Cover and chill for at least 4 hours or overnight.

Heat remaining ½ cup heavy cream in a 1-quart saucepan to boiling. Remove saucepan from heat and add chocolate chips, stirring until mixture is smooth. Let chocolate mixture cool for 15 to 20 minutes or until cool to touch. Pour cooked chocolate mixture evenly over chilled pie. Chill for 30 minutes more or until chocolate mixture is set.

Serves 8
Complexity: Easy

About the Recipe
My daughter's favorite birthday treat!

Creamy Peach Pie

Linda Ochenrider
Principal, Leasure Elementary School/Goodwill Board Member

¾ cup sugar
¼ cup flour
¼ teaspoon salt
¼ teaspoon nutmeg
3 cups peeled and sliced peaches
9-inch unbaked pie shell
1 cup heavy cream

Preheat oven to 400º. Combine dry ingredients. Add peaches and toss. Spoon into pie shell. Pour heavy cream over top. Bake until firm, about 35 to 45 minutes. Cool well before serving.

Serves 8 to 10
Complexity: Easy

About the Recipe

This is my mom's peach pie recipe which never "sleeps!" It's eaten before we all go to bed and is a staple at summer picnics.

Caramelized Orange Tart with Blackberry Puree

Cathy McCartan

Print Consultant, Modern Press Inc.

Crust:
1½ cups plus 3 tablespoons all-purpose flour
½ cup powdered sugar
¼ teaspoon salt
½ cup plus 3 tablespoons chilled unsalted butter, cut into ½-inch pieces
1 large egg, beaten
2 teaspoons (approximately) ice water

Filling:
4 large eggs
1 cup sugar
½ cup orange juice
2 tablespoons fresh lemon juice
2 teaspoons grated orange peel
¼ cup whipping cream
2 tablespoons powdered sugar
Blackberry Puree (Recipe appears on page 154.)

Mix flour, powdered sugar, and salt in a food processor. Add butter slowly and cut in, using on/off turns until mixture resembles coarse meal. Mix in beaten egg. Mix in enough ice water by teaspoonfuls to form moist clumps. Gather dough into a ball and then flatten into a disk. Wrap in plastic and refrigerate for at least 30 minutes. (Can be made 1 day ahead. Keep chilled.)

Soften slightly at room temperature before rolling out. Roll out dough on a floured surface to a14-inch round. Roll up dough on rolling pin and transfer to an 11-inch-diameter tart pan with removable bottom. Trim dough to a 1-inch overhang. Fold in overhang to form double-thick sides extending ¼-inch above sides of pan, pressing to adhere. Pierce crust with a fork in several places. Freeze for 30 minutes.

Preheat oven to 375°. Bake crust until set and light golden, about 18 minutes, piercing with a fork if crust bubbles. Cool completely.

Blend eggs and next 4 ingredients in processor. Add cream and blend until smooth. Pour into cooled crust. Bake tart until filling is set, about 25 minutes. Cool. (Can be made 1 day ahead. Cover and refrigerate.)

Preheat broiler. Cut out a 12-inch round of foil. Cut out center of foil, leaving a 2-inch-wide circle. Place foil circle atop tart, covering crust edges. Dust center of tart with powdered sugar. Broil until sugar melts and is golden, about 1 minute, watching closely and rotating tart for even broiling. Transfer pan to rack. Remove foil circle.

Cool tart for at least 30 minutes. Remove pan sides. Serve tart slightly warm or at room temperature with blackberry puree.

Serves 8 to 12
Complexity: Difficult

About the Recipe

A crowd-pleasing dessert that pairs creamy orange custard with tart blackberry puree. This is a wonderful summer dessert when blackberries are plentiful.

Individual Cheese Cakes

Kristin Strouss
Goodwill Staff

20 cupcake liners
20 Nabisco Vanilla Wafers
2 8-ounce packages cream cheese
½ cup sugar
1 teaspoon vanilla
3 eggs

Preheat oven to 350º. Place cupcake liners in cupcake baking pans. Place one wafer in each liner, round side up.

Mix remaining ingredients together and place about 2 tablespoons on top of each wafer.

Bake for about 17 minutes. Cool for 1 hour.

Serves 20
Complexity: Easy

About the Recipe
If you would like, you can use any flavor pie filling — cherry, blueberry, strawberry — to top it off.

White Chocolate Bread Pudding

David Leo Banks

Executive Chef, Harry's Savoy Grill

1 24-inch loaf stale French bread
6½ cups whipping cream
2 cups milk
1 cup sugar
28 ounces white chocolate, broken into small pieces
4 whole eggs
15 egg yolks
1 ounce dark chocolate, grated into shavings

Preheat oven to 350°.

Peel hard outer bread crust off loaf with a knife or vegetable peeler. (Bread must be stale to peel.) Cut into 1-inch thick cubes. (If the bread is not stale, cut into 1-inch-thick slices, dry in a 275° oven, then cut into cubes.)

In a large saucepan, heat 6 cups whipping cream, milk, and sugar over medium heat. When hot, remove from heat and add 20 ounces white chocolate pieces. Stir until melted.

Combine whole eggs and egg yolks in a mixing bowl. Slowly pour hot cream mixture in a steady stream into eggs, whipping eggs as you pour.

Place bread cubes in a 12 x 9 x 2-inch pan. Pour half the egg mixture over bread. Use fingers to press bread into mixture so that it absorbs the liquid and becomes soggy. Pour in remaining mixture. Cover pan with aluminum foil and bake for 1 hour. Remove foil and bake for an additional 30 minutes until set and golden brown.

Bring remaining ½ cup whipping cream to a boil in a small saucepan. Remove from heat and add remaining 8 ounces white chocolate. Stir until completely melted and smooth. Spoon over bread pudding. Garnish with grated dark chocolate.

Serves 12
Complexity: Moderate

About the Recipe

This recipe was given to Harry's by Tee Martin of the Palace Cafe in New Orleans, LA. Tee is related to the famous Brennan family, owners of Commander's Palace.

Harry's Crème Brûlee

David Leo Banks
Executive Chef, Harry's Savoy Grill

1 quart heavy cream
½ cup white sugar
2 tablespoons pure vanilla extract
8 egg yolks, whisked gently
Light brown sugar
White sugar

Preheat oven 300°.

Heat cream, sugar, and vanilla to 170° and slowly pour into egg yolks, stirring gently. Strain mixture and skim off any foam or froth from top. Pour into 6 oven-proof ramekins and bake in a water bath for 30 to 40 minutes or until just set. Do not let boil or mixture will curdle. Baking time will vary depending on depth of ramekin.

Remove ramekins from oven. Sprinkle with equal parts light brown sugar and white sugar. Heat broiler. Place ramekins under broiler and cook until sugar caramelizes. (This will work better if sugar is dried out for a few days and then ground in a food processor.)

Serves 6
Complexity: Moderate

About the Recipe

My version of crème brûlee was contrived from 3 other recipes — a classic Escoffier recipe, Craig Claiborne's, and Paul Bocuse's — and tweaked to fit Harry's.

Cream Puffs

Clifford M. Brumbaugh

Major League Baseball Player, Chicago White Sox

1 cup water
1 stick butter
1 cup flour
4 large eggs
1 pint heavy whipping cream
1 cup milk
1 large package Jello Instant Pudding

Preheat oven to 400°. Bring water and butter to a boil in a medium pot. Remove from heat. Add flour. Add eggs, one egg at a time, and mix well. Drop by approximately 1 teaspoon mounds onto a slightly greased cookie sheet. Bake on top shelf of oven for 10 minutes. Lower heat to 350° and move tray to bottom shelf of oven. Cook for 20 more minutes. Remove from tray and cool.

Mix together cream, milk, and pudding mix with a hand mixer until thick. Chill for 30 minutes.

Cut puffs in half horizontally and fill with cream mixture.

Yields 2 dozen
Complexity: Moderate

About Goodwill

Typing was a necessary skill taught in early training programs, but Goodwill's Computerized Office Skills Training Program has replaced it. During the five-month program, students learn office and computer skills. [Employee at the Goodwill Center's computer lab assists a student.]

Zucchini Bread

Mark Weischedel
Past Goodwill Board Member

3 eggs
2 cups grated uncooked zucchini, including skin and seeds if soft
2 cups sugar
1 cup oil (see variations)
3 teaspoons vanilla extract
3 cups flour
3 teaspoons cinnamon
1 teaspoon salt
1 teaspoon baking soda
¼ teaspoon baking powder
1 cup chopped nuts

Preheat oven to 350º. Grease and flour a 9 x 5 x 3-inch loaf pan or up to six mini loaf pans.

Beat eggs in a large mixing bowl until fluffy. Add zucchini, sugar, oil, and vanilla and mix well. Combine dry ingredients in a separate bowl. Gradually beat into wet ingredients. Add nuts. Bake for 50 to 60 minutes or until bread begins to separate from side of pan. (For mini loaf pans, reduce baking time by 5 to 10 minutes.) Remove bread from pan(s) and cool completely on rack.

Serves 8 to 12
Complexity: Easy

Variations: For very large zucchinis, remove tough skin and large, hardened seeds. Reduce sugar to 1 or 1½ cups for a low-sugar recipe. Using less sugar will produce a snack-type bread; full amount of sugar will be more like a dessert. Substitute ½ cup each of apple sauce and oil in place of 1 cup oil for a low-fat recipe. Add ¼ to ½ cup raisins or chopped fresh fruit. If using raisins or other dried fruit, be sure fruit is not overly dry (moisten dried fruit with a little water in the microwave) to avoid making the bread too dry.

About the Recipe

This is a very versatile recipe from my mother-in-law, Judy Hannan. We eat it year round, in all sorts of variations. It can serve as a coffee cake, snack, or dessert. It's nice warmed or toasted with a little butter, apple butter or jelly, or just by itself. If you follow the low-sugar and/ or low-fat recipes, it's very nutritious.

Rhubarb Crunch

Patricia D. Beebe

President/CEO, Food Bank of Delaware

1 cup flour
1 cup oatmeal
1 cup brown sugar
½ cup butter
4 cups cut up rhubarb
1 cup sugar
1 cup water
2 tablespoons cornstarch
Dash of vanilla extract

Combine flour, oatmeal, and brown sugar. Cut in butter until crumbs form. Press into baking dish, reserving a few crumbs for the top. Add rhubarb.

Preheat oven to 350°. Combine remaining ingredients in a saucepan. Cook until thick and clear. Pour over rhubarb. Sprinkle with remaining crumbs. Bake for about 45 minutes.

Serves 6
Complexity: Moderate

About the Recipe

This recipe comes from my Aunt Eliza and was handed down from the great Norwegian cooks. She was my father's sister and would always be remembered for her porch swing and great food.

Cranberry Dream Bars

Patricia D. Beebe

President/CEO, Food Bank of Delaware

2 cups flour
¾ cup powdered sugar
1 cup butter
4 eggs
2 cups sugar
½ cup flour
¼ teaspoon salt
4 cups chopped cranberries

Preheat oven to 350°. Combine flour and powdered sugar. Cut in butter until crumbs form. Press into bottom of 15 x 10 x 1-inch jelly-roll pan. Bake for 15 minutes.

Blend eggs, sugar, flour, and salt until smooth. Fold in cranberries. Spread over hot crust. Bake for 25 minutes until filling is lightly browned. Cool and cut into bars or squares.

Yields approximately 60 squares
Complexity: Moderate

About the Recipe

Comes from my sister, Carrie Anderson, who lives in Northern Wisconsin. It was passed down from Native Americans. Great holiday dessert.

Magic Cookie Bars

Patricia D. Beebe

President/CEO, Food Bank of Delaware

½ cup melted butter
1¼ cups graham cracker crumbs
1 cup chopped nuts
1 cup semi-sweet chocolate pieces
1⅓ cups flaked coconut
1 15-ounce can Borden Sweetened Condensed Milk

Preheat oven to 350°. Pour melted butter into bottom of a 9 x 13-inch pan. Spread graham cracker crumbs evenly over butter, mix, and press into place. Add a layer of chopped nuts and press into place. Add a layer of chocolate chips and then coconut. Cover with sweetened condensed milk. Bake for 25 minutes or until lightly browned on top. Cool before cutting into bars.

Yields: about 2 dozen
Complexity: Easy

About the Recipe

A favorite of both my children, Kyle and Lauren and many of their friends who frequently ask me to make these treats. They are quick to eat many of these at family gatherings.

Chewey Gooey's

Beverly Brainard Fleming
Data Analyst, Astrazeneca

1 14-ounce bag caramels
⅔ cup evaporated milk
1 box German Chocolate cake mix
¾ cup melted margarine or butter
1 cup coarsely chopped pecans
1 6-ounce bag or 1 cup semi-sweet chocolate chips

Preheat oven to 350°. Grease and flour a 13 x 9-inch cake pan.

Melt caramels with ⅓ cup evaporated milk in a double boiler. In a large mixing bowl, blend remaining ⅓ cup evaporated milk, cake mix, margarine, and pecans until moistened.

Press less than half of cake mixture into pan. Bake for 6 minutes. Sprinkle chocolate chips evenly over baked mixture and pour caramel mixture over chips. Cover with remaining cake mixture. If you can't spread it, flatten between hands and place on top "patchwork style." Bake for 15 minutes. Cool before cutting into squares.

Serves 1 to 12 persons depending on their appetite.
Complexity: Moderate

About the Recipe
Big kids, little kids, young, and old all love these yummy bars. I could never make enough.

Anisette Sponge & Toast

Colleen Morrone
Goodwill Staff

4 large eggs
1 cup sugar
1 cup vegetable oil
3 cups sifted flour
2 teaspoons baking powder
¼ teaspoon baking soda
¼ teaspoon salt
1 teaspoon vanilla extract
1 teaspoon anise extract
1 cup chopped nuts, optional

Preheat oven to 350º. Grease 3 or 4 metal ice cube trays. Beat eggs until light in color. Beat in sugar and oil. Add dry ingredients and beat. Mix in extracts and nuts. Spoon batter equally into trays. Bake for 28 minutes. Let cool, then remove from trays and cut into ½-inch slices.

For anisette toast, toast slices on a cookie sheet in a 350º oven for a few minutes on each side until delicate brown in color.

Yields approximately 6 dozen cookies
Complexity: Easy

About the Recipe

Great for breakfast or after dinner with a cup of coffee. This is one of my favorite recipes from my Aunt Betty.

Grandma's Sugar Cookies

Susan Irby
Owner/Chef, Cooking with Susan

½ cup margarine or butter
1 cup sugar
1 medium egg
½ teaspoon salt
2 teaspoons baking powder
2 cups flour
½ teaspoon vanilla
¾ cup confectioners' sugar
3 teaspoon water
3 drops food coloring (your choice of color)

Preheat oven to 400°. Cream together margarine and sugar. Blend in egg. Sift together salt, baking powder, and flour. Blend in vanilla. Roll out dough with rolling pin onto wax paper. Cut with cookie cutters of your choice. Lay cookies on an ungreased cookie sheet. Bake for 8 to 10 minutes.

Combine confectioners' sugar, water, and food coloring to make a glaze. While cookies are warm, brush with glaze using a pastry brush.

Serves 12
Complexity: Easy

About the Recipe

A family favorite from my cookbook, "Cooking with Susan: Southern Family Favorites." This was my grandmother Monnie's recipe. She was a true "Southern Belle" who loved sharing and traveling. Now, I have many, many stories to tell about making these little charmers. My sister and I used to fight over who would get to lick the dough off the beaters. Fortunately, we did not really fight over them; and there were two beaters, so we each got our own. My favorite part about making these was choosing which cookie cutter to use! We had one Santa cutter that part of his shoes always came off. He would turn out funny looking because I would "smash" it back on before baking. My mother, sister, and I made these cookies on all occasions, especially during Christmas time!

Snickerdoodles

Barbara Maddams
Goodwill Staff

1 cup butter, softened
1½ cups sugar
2 eggs
2¾ cups Gold Medal flour, measured by sifting
2 teaspoons cream of tartar
1 teaspoon baking soda
½ teaspoon salt
2 tablespoons sugar
2 teaspoons cinnamon

Heat oven to 400°. Mix butter, sugar, and eggs thoroughly. In a separate bowl, combine flour, cream of tartar, baking soda, and salt. Add to wet ingredients. Roll into balls the size of small walnuts.

Combine sugar and cinnamon. Roll dough balls in cinnamon and sugar mixture. Place 2 inches apart on an ungreased baking sheet. Bake for 8 to 10 minutes. (These cookies puff up at first, then flatten out).

Note: For best results, refrigerate dough overnight.

Yields 5 dozen cookies
Complexity: Easy

About the Recipe

My favorite part of this recipe is eating the dough rolled in the cinnamon before it was cooked. My mom would always try to bake these when she knew I would not be home so I would not eat all of the dough before she made the cookies.

Chocolate Kiss Cookies

Janet Doto
Goodwill Staff

1 15-ounces package Duncan Hines Golden Sugar Cookie Mix
½ cup Hershey's Cocoa
1 egg
2 tablespoons water
¾ cup finely chopped nuts
1 9-ounce bag Hershey's Kisses chocolates

Heat oven to 350°. Combine cookie mix and the enclosed flavor packet, cocoa, egg and water in a medium bowl. Mix with a spoon or fork until thoroughly blended. Shape dough into 1-inch balls. Roll balls in nuts. Place on an ungreased cookie sheet. Bake for about 8 minutes. Immediately press Kiss into center of each warm cookie. Cool slightly, then remove from cookie sheet to rack and cool completely.

Yields: 3 dozen
Complexity: Easy

About Goodwill

The Food Service Skills Training is a unique partnership program between Goodwill Industries and the Food Bank of Delaware. During the 12-week program, students learn and develop skills needed to enter the food service industry. Students train in a state-of-the-art, "working" kitchen and computer lab/classroom. The success of the program has inspired Goodwill Industries International and America's Second Harvest to join forces and offer similar programs throughout the nation.

Red Raspberry Cookies

Beverley Brainard Fleming
Data Analyst, Astrazeneca

1 cup butter or margarine, softened
1½ cups sugar
1 egg
1½ teaspoons vanilla extract
3½ cups all-purpose flour, stirred before measuring
1 teaspoon salt
½ to ¾ cup Smucker's Red Raspberry Preserves
½ cup finely ground hazelnuts, optional
Confectioners' sugar

In a large bowl, cream together butter and sugar until light and fluffy. Add egg and vanilla and beat well. Stir in flour and salt. Stir well to make a smooth dough. (If batter gets too hard to handle, mix with hands.) Refrigerate about 2 hours.

Preheat oven to 375°. Lightly grease baking sheets. Cut dough in half. Roll out one half on a lightly floured board to about a ¼-inch of thickness. Cut with a 2½-inch cookie cutter. Place on baking sheets.

Roll out remaining dough. Cut with a 2½-inch cutter with a hole in the middle. Place on baking sheets. Bake for about 8 to 10 minutes or until lightly browned. Cool for about 30 minutes.

To serve, spread preserves on plain cookie and top with a cookie with hole. Sprinkle with hazelnuts and/or confectioners' sugar.

Complexity: Easy

About the Recipe
A longtime favorite of friends and family. These can also be made in heart shapes for Valentine's Day!

Applesauce Jumbles
with Brown Butter Glaze

Theresa Gray
Goodwill Staff

¾ cup applesauce
2 eggs
½ cup shortening
3¼ cups all-purpose flour
1½ cups brown sugar, packed
1 teaspoon cinnamon
1 teaspoon vanilla
½ teaspoon salt
½ teaspoon baking soda
¼ teaspoon ground cloves
1 cup chopped walnuts
1 cup raisins, optional

Glaze:
⅓ cup margarine or butter
2 cups powdered sugar
1½ teaspoons vanilla
2 to 4 tablespoons hot water

Preheat oven to 375°. Mix all ingredients except glaze. (If dough is soft, cover and refrigerate.) Drop dough by level tablespoons 2 inches apart onto ungreased cookie sheet. Bake for 10 minutes or until almost no indentation remains when touched with finger. Cool.

To make glaze, heat margarine over low heat until golden brown; remove from heat. Stir in powdered sugar and vanilla. Beat in hot water until smooth. Spread jumbles with glaze.

Yields 4 to 5 dozen cookies
Complexity: Easy

About the Recipe
I first made these cookies when I was snowed in with my kids one weekend. These are great cookies to take to the office!

Dad's Kruschiki

Karen E. Kanich
Goodwill Staff

1 teaspoon sugar
½ teaspoon baking powder
½ teaspoon salt
2 tablespoons vegetable oil
½ cup orange juice or Christian Bros. brandy
3 eggs, well beaten
3 to 4 cups sifted flour
Powdered sugar

Add sugar, baking powder, salt, oil, and orange juice to beaten eggs and blend. Gradually add enough flour to form dough. Mix until all ingredients are fully incorporated, leaving sides and bottom of mixing bowl "clean."

Knead until smooth, keeping hands dusted with flour to prevent "sticking." Place a handful of dough on a floured cutting board or wax paper. Roll paper thin with floured rolling pin until you can almost see your hand through it.

Cut dough into 1 x 3-inch strips. Cut a 1-inch slit in the middle of each strip. Tuck one end of strip through middle slit and work gently out into a "bow." Fry in about 1 inch of vegetable oil until golden in color. While still warm, sprinkle with powdered sugar.

Serves 6 to 8
Complexity: Moderate

About the Recipe

Dad made this a Christmas Eve ritual. He would line all five of us children up assembly-line style, and each of us would enjoy those few hours together making the best dessert in the whole wide world. I did the same with my daughters and look forward to participating with my grandchildren in keeping a family tradition alive, making this the fourth generation in a row to spend Christmas Eve covered in flour.

Frozen Bananas

Janet Doto
Goodwill Staff

3 large ripe bananas
9 wooden ice cream sticks
2 cups (12-ounce package) Hershey's Semi-Sweet Chocolate Chips
2 tablespoons shortening
1½ cups coarsely chopped unsalted roasted peanuts

Peel bananas and cut each into thirds. Insert wooden stick into each banana piece and place on a wax paper covered tray. Cover and freeze until firm.

Melt chocolate chips and shortening in a double boiler over hot, but not boiling, water. Remove bananas from freezer just before dipping. Dip each banana into warm chocolate, covering completely. Allow excess to drip off. Immediately roll in peanuts. Cover and return to freezer. Serve frozen.

Serves 9
Complexity: Easy

About Goodwill

No disability is too great when a person's desire to succeed is so strong. [Photo from Morgan Memorial Goodwill Industries, Inc.]

Dixie's Delights

Kristen Tosh
Music Teacher, George Read Middle School

3 or 4 overripe bananas
½ cup peanut butter
1 cup wheat germ, crunchy cereal, or chopped peanuts
Nonstick spray

Place bananas and peanut butter in a large mixing bowl. Microwave for 1 minute, stir well, and microwave again for 2 minutes. Blend ingredients so that you have a nice consistency and no lumps. (You may want to add more peanut butter if the mixture is too thin.) Refrigerate for 2 hours or until cool to the touch.

Evenly coat the bottom of a large pie plate with nonstick spray. Place wheat germ in a shallow bowl. Scoop out a teaspoon of banana mixture and roll it into a ball. Roll ball over wheat germ until coated evenly. Place ball in greased pie plate. Make sure treats are not touching.

Freeze the pie plate of treats for 2 hours. Remove from freezer and store in an airtight plastic container. Enjoy!

Serves 4
Complexity: Easy

About the Recipe

When you find yourself with some overripe bananas, don't throw them away! Make this tasty little treat for the dog, the kids, or yourself!

Bru

NOT CHARITY, BUT A CHANCE!

nch

Christmas Brunch Souffle

Linda Ochenrider

Principal, Leasure Elementary School/Goodwill Board Member

1 stick butter, softened
9 slices Pepperidge Farm Toasting White Bread
½ pound sharp cheese, grated
1 pound bacon, fried and cut into pieces
6 eggs
3 cups milk
½ teaspoon salt
¼ teaspoon pepper

Generously butter bread and cut into cubes. Place in a 9½ x 11-inch greased baking dish. Sprinkle with cheese, then bacon. Place eggs, milk, salt, and pepper in blender or large bowl and mix well. Pour over bread, cheese, and bacon. Refrigerate overnight.
When ready to bake, preheat oven to 350º. Bake for 40 to 45 minutes.

Serves 12
Complexity: Easy

About the Recipe

This was our standard Christmas morning brunch when my son was little. After he left home for college, this was always on his "mom, please make ... when I come home to visit."

Finnish Pancakes

Patricia D. Beebe
President/CEO, Food Bank of Delaware

3 eggs, well beaten
2 cups milk
⅓ cup sugar
1 teaspoon salt
1½ cups flour
2 tablespoons oil

Preheat oven to 400°. Mix together eggs, milk, sugar, and salt. Add flour and oil.
Bake in a greased jelly-roll pan for 30 minutes. Cut into squares and serve hot.

Serves 4
Complexity: Easy

About the Recipe

This recipe was copied from listening to the radio from my mother in Iron Wood, Michigan. It quickly became a family favorite and remains a brunch favorite at the Beebe home.

Gourmet Pancakes

Beverley Brainard Fleming
Data Analyst, Astrazeneca

2 eggs, lightly beaten
½ cup milk
½ cup flour
⅛ teaspoon nutmeg
8 tablespoons butter
Confectioners' sugar
1 lemon, sliced
Honey

Preheat oven to 450°. Combine eggs, milk, flour, and nutmeg and beat lightly but leave lumps in the batter.

Heat 2 ovenproof 8-inch or 9-inch skillets on stove top. Place 4 tablespoons butter in each skillet and melt. When butter is melted but not browned, pour batter into skillets. Transfer skillets to oven. Reduce temperature to 425°. Bake for 15 to 20 minutes until pancakes are raised and brown.

Transfer pancakes to warm serving plates. Sprinkle with confectioners' sugar. Garnish with lemon slices and honey.

Serves 2
Complexity: Easy

About the Recipe

This is a crowd pleaser. Beach house friends and family love this recipe! For a summer treat, serve with fresh strawberries, peaches, or raspberries flavored with Kirsch.

Buckwheat Cakes

John Eakin
Friend of Goodwill Industries

1½ cups buckwheat flour
2 rounded tablespoons sugar
2 heaping teaspoons baking powder
⅛ teaspoon salt
1 egg
3 tablespoons melted butter or margarine
1 cup milk or more if necessary to make batter desired consistency

Sift and mix together flour, sugar, baking powder, and salt. Whisk egg and mix into dry ingredients. Add melted butter and stir well.

Cook on a greased hot iron skillet until bubbles form all over each cake, then turn and brown other side. Serve hot with butter and maple syrup.

Serves 4
Complexity: Easy

About the Recipe
This recipe was written by John Eakin's mother and published in her church's cookbook in 1952.

Strawberry-Ricotta Crepes

Antoinette DiMatteo
Office Manager, Delaware Design Co.

2 pounds ricotta cheese
½ cup sugar
5 teaspoons plus ½ cup apricot preserves
½ teaspoon cinnamon
½ teaspoon freshly ground nutmeg
20 Nutmeg Crepes (Recipe appears on page 141.)
¼ cup Cointreau
1 pint fresh strawberries, hulled and sliced
Powdered sugar

Combine ricotta cheese, sugar, 5 teaspoons apricot preserves, cinnamon, and nutmeg in a medium bowl and mix well with a fork.

Spoon 2 tablespoons mixture down the center of one crepe. Bring up two opposite sides and overlap on filling. Arrange, seam side down, in a serving dish. Repeat with remaining cheese mixture and crepes.

Heat remaining ½ cup preserves and Cointreau in a small saucepan over medium heat until warmed through. Arrange sliced strawberries over crepes, then pour on sauce. Sprinkle with powdered sugar and serve.

Serves 10
Complexity: Moderate

About the Recipe
We were invited to a friend's house for dinner, and I offered to make the dessert. I made crepes, adding nutmeg to the batter, and came up with this recipe. It was a great success, and I have been making this elegant dish for parties ever since.

Nutmeg Crepes

Antoinette DiMatteo
Office Manager, Delaware Design Co.

3 cups pastry flour, sifted
2 cups milk
⅛ teaspoon freshly ground nutmeg
4 eggs, separated
¼ cup sugar
1 cup melted butter

Whisk flour, milk, and nutmeg in a large bowl. Add yolks, one at a time, mixing well after each addition. Whisk in sugar. Gradually whisk in melted butter. Beat whites in a small bowl or electric mixer until stiff but not dry. Fold whites into batter.

Heat a crepe pan or small 6-inch skillet over medium-high heat. Working quickly, add about 3 tablespoons batter to one edge of pan, tilting and swirling until bottom is covered with a thin layer of batter. Pour any excess batter back into bowl. Return pan to medium-high heat. Loosen edge of crepe with a small spatula or knife, discarding any pieces clinging to sides of pan. Cook until bottom is lightly browned. Turn or flip over and cook second side until lightly browned. Slide onto plate. Top with a sheet of waxed paper or foil. Repeat with remaining batter, stirring occasionally.

Yields twenty 6-inch crepes
Complexity: Moderate

About Goodwill

Banking on the Future! In 2002, Goodwill Industries began their first training program for youth between the ages of 16 and 21 – Youth Banking and Financial Training. [Students learn to deal with monetary situations.]

Barb's Pumpkin Roll

Beverley Brainard Fleming
Data Analyst, Astrazeneca

⅔ cup canned pumpkin
3 eggs
1 cup sugar
¾ cup flour
1 teaspoon baking soda
1 teaspoon cinnamon
8 ounces cream cheese
4 tablespoons butter, softened
1 teaspoon vanilla
1 cup confectioners' sugar

Preheat oven to 375°. Combine pumpkin, eggs, sugar, flour, baking soda, and cinnamon. Pour onto a greased 16 x 14-inch cookie sheet. Bake for 11 minutes. Remove from oven and let sit for 15 minutes. Cover with foil and flip over. Roll in foil and refrigerate for 15 minutes.

Mix together cream cheese, butter, vanilla, and confectioners' sugar. Unroll pumpkin roll and cover with cream cheese mixture. Reroll and slice to serve.

Serves 6 to 8
Complexity: Easy

About the Recipe
This is so wonderful in the fall or Christmastime. It is yummy for brunch, but also a great dessert.

Sour Cream Coffee Cake

Roz Bratt

Owner/Baker, Homemade Goodies by Roz

1 stick margarine
½ cup vegetable shortening
2 cups sugar
3 large eggs
3 cups flour
3 teaspoons baking powder
½ teaspoon baking soda
1 cup sour cream
1½ teaspoons almond extract
1½ teaspoons vanilla extract
½ cup chopped nuts
2 teaspoons cinnamon

Preheat oven to 350°. Grease a 10-inch tube pan. Cream together margarine, shortening, and 1½ cup sugar. Add eggs and mix for 2 minutes. Combine flour, baking powder, and baking soda in a separate bowl. Add dry ingredients to wet, alternating with sour cream. Stir in almond and vanilla extracts.

In a separate bowl, mix together remaining sugar, nuts, and cinnamon.

Spoon one-third batter into pan. Sprinkle with one-third crumb mixture. Repeat two more times. Bake for 60 minutes or until inserted toothpick comes out clean.

Yields 12 to 14 slices
Complexity: Easy

About Goodwill

In 2003, Arline Docherty, Executive Assistant, Goodwill Industries of Delaware & Delaware County, Inc. (GIDDC), was the first recipient of GIDDC's Graduate Staff of the Year Award. She also won Goodwill Industries International's (GII) Edgar J. Helms' Graduate Staff of the Year Award. Arline, a graduate of Goodwill's Computerized Office Skills Training Program, is the first GIDDC employee or graduate to win a GII award. See Arline's Vieux Larré Scampi recipe on page 77. [Picture courtesy of Fred Bourdon Photography.]

Toasted Bananas

Bob Older

President, Creative Travel/Goodwill Board Member

1 large, firm ripe banana
2 teaspoons lemon juice
2 flour tortillas
2 tablespoons sugar
1 teaspoon cinnamon
⅛ teaspoon nutmeg
2 tablespoons milk
Chocolate sauce, optional

Preheat oven to 400°. Peel banana and cut in half lengthwise. Coat banana with lemon juice to prevent browning. Place each slice at one end of each tortilla. Combine sugar, cinnamon, and nutmeg in a small bowl. Sprinkle part of sugar mixture over bananas, reserving remainder for later. Carefully roll tortillas and secure with toothpicks. Brush tortillas lightly with milk and sprinkle remaining sugar mixture on top. Place in a well-greased baking dish and bake for 15 minutes. Serve immediately. If desired, serve chocolate sauce with toasted bananas.

Serves 2
Complexity: Easy

About Goodwill

During training, students attend Goodwill "life skills" classes, which teach team building, financial planning, time management, and a host of other skills needed to enter the workforce.

Heart Scones with Blackberry Butter

Beverley Brainard Fleming

Data Analyst, Astrazeneca

4½ cups sifted all-purpose flour
2 teaspoons baking powder
½ tablespoon baking soda
Pinch of salt
2 tablespoons sugar
½ pound (2 sticks) cold unsalted butter, cut into small pieces
1 to 1¼ cups heavy cream
1 egg
¼ cup light cream
Blackberry Butter (Recipe appears on page 154.)

Preheat the oven to 375º. Sift the dry ingredients into a large mixing bowl. Cut butter into the mixture with a pastry blender or with two knives until mixture resembles coarse meal. (Butter cut in can also be done in a food processor, using half the flour mixture. Then add mixture to the remaining flour in bowl before adding cream.) Mixing lightly with your fingers, add heavy cream just until dough holds together. Wrap in plastic and chill for about ½ hour. Roll dough into a circle: ½-inch thick for small scones and ¾-inch thick for larger ones. Using a biscuit or cookie cutter, cut dough into various shapes.

Butter a large sheet and place scones on it. Combine egg and light cream in a bowl and brush tops of scones with the mixture. Bake until golden brown and puffed, 13 to 15 minutes. Serve with blackberry butter.

Yields approximately 40 scones
Complexity: Moderate

About the Recipe

Great for afternoon tea, brunch, or a special treat for your Valentine!

This ar

MILWAUKEE EDITION

VOL. 2. MARCH, APRIL, MAY, 1924 No. 3.

THE

GOODWILL INDUSTRIES

INDEPENDENCE
CHARACTER
TRAINING
WORK
SHELTER
FOOD

GOODWILL INDUSTRIES

DESIGNED BY THE GOODWILL INDUSTRIES OF SAN DIEGO, CALIFORNIA

NOT CHARITY, BUT A CHANCE!

d That

Spiced Olives

Dorothy W. Webb
Retired

1 7-ounce jar small pimento stuffed olives
1¼ teaspoons crushed oregano
½ teaspoon paprika
1 bay leaf
1 teaspoon minced garlic (about 1 medium clove)
White vinegar

Drain liquid from olives and reserve. Remove about one-quarter of the olives from the jar and set aside. Add seasonings to jar. Add a little vinegar, cover, and shake to blend. Replace removed olives. Add enough vinegar to fill jar halfway. Cover and shake again. Fill jar to brim with reserved olive liquid. Cover and shake again to blend. Refrigerate for 7 to 10 days before using. Shake 2 to 3 times during this time.

Yields: 1 jar
Complexity: Easy

About the Recipe

These olives are good anytime. Especially good in picadillo. Super to put on sliced tomatoes with a little of the liquid. The brine can be used in many dishes in place of regular vinegar. Martini lovers like one or two in their cocktail. Once you try them, you will always have a jar in your refrigerator. Also makes a nice gift. Just tie a ribbon around the jar and add a card with hints for use.

Gin Raisins
My Italian Mom's Medicinal Recipe
for Aches and Pains

Anita M. Cleaver

Administrative Manager, Creative Financial Concepts, Inc./Goodwill Board Member

1 10-ounce box golden raisins (only yellow, white, or golden raisins)
Gin

Place raisins in a large GLASS jar with a tight lid. Fill jar with gin to about one inch above the raisins and screw lid on tight.

Check jar no less than weekly by turning it upside down to eliminate any bubbles and to determine that the raisins are absorbing the gin. If the gin level falls below the surface of the top raisins, be sure to add more gin, maintaining a level at least a half inch above the raisins. Let raisins absorb gin for 3 to 4 weeks before using.

Take 9 raisins (not 8 and not 10, ONLY 9) before going to bed each night. Be sure to refill the gin whenever the level begins to fall below the top of the raisins. Of course, these raisins should never be consumed if you are taking any medication that would interfere with alcohol.

Complexity: Easy

About the Recipe

My mother, Giovanna (Jennie) Pologruto, emigrated from Genoa, Italy, through Ellis Island as a young girl. She and my dad settled in Philadelphia and later moved to a small farm in New Jersey, where I was raised along with my brothers and sisters. We raised chickens, selling the eggs, and cultivated fresh fruits and vegetables. We also had a grape vineyard, my dad's hobby. At the end of the season everything was picked and was turned into something edible, including the grapes: nothing ever went to waste. Needless to say, this is just one of the many "Old Italian Recipes" my mother has passed down to me. It is my pleasure to share this recipe and the memory of this old custom with Goodwill Industries of Delaware.

Beef Jerky

Linda Dyson
Past Board Member Spouse

3 to 5 pounds lean beef (flank or round steak)
1 cup warm water
¼ cup soy sauce
2 tablespoons liquid smoke
1 tablespoon salt (hickory smoked, garlic, or onion)
¾ teaspoon black pepper (or to taste)
Oregano, basil, thyme, and marjoram, sprinkled liberally

Semi-freeze meat for easier slicing. Cut with the grain into ¼-inch-thick strips measuring 4 to 6 inches long. Remove all fat and gristle.

Combine warm water and soy sauce, then add liquid smoke. Add remaining ingredients. Layer meat with marinade in a large bowl and refrigerate for at least 8 hours.

Bring a pan of salted water to boil. Using tongs, dip each strip into water for about 15 seconds. (This will blanch the meat and destroy surface bacteria.) Place strips on cookie trays.

Set oven to lowest temperature possible. Place trays on oven racks and bake for 10 to 16 hours. Keep door propped ajar to allow moisture to escape. Meat will dehydrate with the slow heat and will shrivel.

When finished baking, allow meat to cool before eating. Store in airtight jars.

Complexity: Moderate

About the Recipe

While living in Houston, Texas, in the '70s, I discovered a recipe for beef jerky in an old camping magazine. After reworking it, I chose Christmas Eve to establish a tradition for my son which sent him off to bed, not with "visions of sugar plums dancing in his head" but instead, the savory rich aroma of jerky drying out in our ovens. It was Christmas morning breakfast.

Bob's Bam

Robert R. Hopkins
Goodwill Staff

Salt
Pepper (black or white)
Garlic powder
Onion powder
Paprika

Mix together equal amounts of each ingredient in a bowl. (Purchase 1-ounce jars of seasonings in the supermarket or use whatever amount you choose.) Refill in original containers or a container of your choice.

Complexity: Easy

About the Recipe

This is the basic recipe for the meat seasoning for a restaurant I used to cook at (name withheld to protect the innocent). It works well for meat, fish, fowl, and pork. Use a funnel to refill jars. Also put a little raw rice in bottles to keep out moisture.

Basic Marinara Sauce

Mark Chew
Owner, Courtney's

3 tablespoons olive oil
½ medium-sized onion, diced
1 clove garlic, minced
10 large, ripe tomatoes, peeled, seeded and chopped
5 leaves fresh basil, chopped
1 teaspoon granulated sugar
Salt and freshly ground pepper to taste

Heat oil in a large, heavy pot over medium heat. Add onions and garlic. Sauté until onions are translucent, about 5 to 8 minutes.

Add tomatoes and simmer, uncovered, for about 45 minutes. Stir often so that tomatoes are broken up and sauce is fairly smooth.

Add basil and sugar. Simmer for 10 minutes. Season to taste with salt and pepper. Sauce may be used immediately or frozen for later use.

Yields 4 cups
Complexity: Easy

Dijon Cream Sauce

Tim Rawlins
Chef, Valle Cucina Italiana Restaurant

½ teaspoon butter
1½ cups heavy cream
Pinch of dried basil
Salt and pepper to taste
2 tablespoons Dijon mustard
Parmesan cheese

Melt butter in a saucepan. Add heavy cream, basil, and salt and pepper to taste. Bring to a boil. Add Dijon mustard and bring to a boil again. Add a sprinkle of Parmesan cheese. Keep warm until ready to serve.

Champagne Mustard Sauce

Tom Hannum
Executive Chef, The Hotel duPont

4 to 5 shallots, chopped
1 cup white wine
1 quart heavy cream
Salt and pepper to taste
½ cup champagne mustard

Place shallots and wine in a saucepan. Bring to a simmer and reduce until liquid is a syrup. Add heavy cream. Continue cooking until liquid is reduced by half. Adjust seasoning with salt and pepper. Strain. Add champagne mustard and stir until warmed through.

Betty Ann's Mushroom Burgundy Gravy

Colleen Morrone
Goodwill Staff

1 tablespoon dried shallots (2, if fresh)
1 tablespoon butter
¼ teaspoon garlic powder
12 ounces mushrooms, sliced
½ cup burgundy wine
2 cans Campbell's Beef Broth (bouillon)
4 tablespoons flour
¼ teaspoon black pepper

Sauté shallots in butter for 1 minute. Add garlic powder. Add sliced mushrooms. Cook until mushrooms have released all their liquid and have started to brown lightly. Add burgundy wine.

In a blender, mix beef broth with flour. Add broth and flour mixture to mushroom mixture. Add black pepper. Bring gravy to a boil, slowly. Continue cooking for at least 5 minutes.

Serve with filet mignon roast or any roasted beef.

Serves: Enough for a roast
Complexity: Easy

Sweet Yellow Pepper Puree

Leo Medisch
Chef, Back Porch Cafe

4 cups Lewes Dairy cream
1 shallot, chopped
2 yellow peppers, peeled and seeded
Salt and white pepper to taste

Cook cream and shallot over medium heat until reduced by half. Place cream, yellow peppers, and salt and white pepper in a food processor fitted with a metal blade and process until smooth. Strain and keep warm until ready to serve.

Blackberry Puree

Cathy McCartan
Print Consultant, Modern Press Inc.

1 16-ounce package frozen unsweetened blackberries, thawed
6 tablespoons sugar

Puree berries and sugar in a processor. Strain through fine sieve; discard seeds. (Can be made 1 day ahead. Cover and chill.)

Makes about 1½ cups

Blackberry Butter

Beverley Brainard Fleming
Data Analyst, Astrazeneca

½ pound unsalted butter, at room temperature
½ cup ripe blackberries, fresh or frozen (thawed and drained)

In a food processor, process butter and berries to a smooth puree. (The butter will have a deep pink color.) Spoon butter into a small serving dish and refrigerate.

Remove from refrigerator 1 hour before serving. Serve, with a small butter spreader, to accompany scones, muffins, toast, etc.

Note: Blackberries can be replaced with ½ cup sliced fresh strawberries, ½ cup fresh raspberries, ⅓ cup plum preserves, or ⅓ cup raspberry preserves.

Index

A

Albertson, Charlotte Ann 101
Alfree III, Charles "Ebbie" 30
Anisette Sponge & Toast 125
Apple
    Applesauce Jumbles 130
    Celery and Apple Salad Dijon 32
Applesauce Jumbles 130
Asian Slaw 36
Asparagus Cashew Rice Pilaf 92
Aunt Fanny's Squash Recipe 100

B

Back Porch Cafe 154
Bacon
    Broccoli Salad 34
    Calico Beans 63
    Christmas Brunch Souffle 136
    Clam Chowder 44
    Smokey Mountain Rice 94
Balzano, Anna C. 15, 59
Bananas
    Dixie's Delights 133
    Frozen Bananas 132
    Toasted Bananas 144
Barb's Pumpkin Roll 142
Barnard Good House 96
Barnes, James 70
Bars
    Chewey Gooey's 124
    Cranberry Dream Bars 122
    Magic Cookie Bars 123
Basic Marinara Sauce 152
Bass
    Chilean Sea Bass Special 71
    Whole Roasted Black Bass in Sea Salt Crust 70
Beans
    Calico Beans 63
    Not-Just-Any-Chili Chili 46
    Sweet Spicy Chili 47
Becca's Blue Ribbon Meat Loaf 62
Beebe, Patricia D. 63, 121, 122, 123, 137
Beef
    Becca's Blue Ribbon Meat Loaf 62
    Calico Beans 63
    Cape Fillet of Beef 61
    Chipped Beef Dip 14
    Jerky 150
    Not-Just-Any-Chili Chili 46
    Sausage Rounds 19
    Sweet Spicy Chili 47
    Taco Toss 64
Betty Ann's Mushroom Burgundy Gravy 153
Blackberry
    Butter 145, 154
    Caramelized Orange Tart with Blackberry Puree 114
    Puree 154
Blood Orange and Fennel Salad 33
Bob's Bam 151
Bratt, Roz 143
Bread
    Bruschetta 20
    Christmas Brunch Souffle 136
    Sausage Rounds 19
    Zucchini Bread 120
Broccoli
    Chicken Casserole 54
    Cream of Broccoli Soup 41
    Salad 34
Brown, Joe 35
Brumbaugh, Clifford M. 119
Bruschetta 20
Brussels Sprouts with Maple Mustard Sauce 101
Buckwheat Cakes 139
Burns, Mickey 112
Butter
    Blackberry Butter 145, 154
    Mrs. Habbersett's Orange Almond Buttercake 107
    Philadelphia German Butter Cake 106

C

Cabbage
    Couscous Marrakesh 95
    Mediterranean Cole Slaw 37
Cakes
    Barb's Pumpkin Roll 142
    Carrot Cake 110
    Fruit Cocktail Cake 109
    Grandma's Pound Cake 108
    Individual Cheese Cakes 116
    Mrs. Habbersett's Orange Almond Buttercake 107
    Philadelphia German Butter Cake 106
    Sour Cream Coffee Cake 143
Calico Beans 63
Cape Fillet of Beef 61
Capiccotti, Marie 109
Caramelized Orange Tart with Blackberry Puree 114
Caribbean Carrots 102
Caribbean Curry Chicken 56
Carrots
    Caribbean Carrots 102
    Couscous Marrakesh 95
    Cream of Broccoli Soup 41
    Medley of Vegetables 98
Casserole
    Chicken 54
    Christmas Brunch Souffle 136
    Easy Chicken and Rice Casserole 53
    Potato 96
    Rhubarb Crunch 121
Castro, Rebecca 55, 62, 64

Celery
   and Apple Salad Dijon 32
   Easy Chicken and Rice Casserole 53
   Medley of Vegetables 98
   Not-What-You'd-Expect Celery Salad 31
Champagne Mustard Sauce 153
Cheddar Cheese and Olive Balls 15
Cheese
   Broccoli Salad 34
   Cheddar Cheese and Olive Balls 15
   Chicken Casserole 54
   Christmas Brunch Souffle 136
   Eggplant Parmesan 78
   Homemade Gnocchi 86
   Macaroni and Cheese 89
   Pasta with Four Cheeses 84
   Pregnancy Pasta 87
   Ravioli with Gorgonzola Fig Cream 85
   Sausage Rounds 19
   Strawberry-Ricotta Crepes 140
   Taco Toss 64
Chew, Mark 23, 24, 40, 79, 88, 152
Chewey Gooey's 124
Chicken
   Cacciatore 59
   Caribbean Curry Chicken 56
   Casserole 54
   Easy Chicken and Rice Casserole 53
   Grilled Caribbean Chicken 57
   Lime Chicken 58
   Rice Stuffed Chicken Breast with Dijon Cream Sauce 52
   Splattered Chicken Pasta 60
   Sticky Chicken 55
   Summer Salad for One 30
Chilean Sea Bass Special 71
Chili
   Not-Just-Any-Chili 46
   Sweet Spicy 47
Chipped Beef Dip 14
Chocolate
   Chewey Gooey's 124
   Frozen Bananas 132
   Kiss Cookies 128
   Magic Cookie Bars 123
   Peanut Butter Pie 112
Christmas Brunch Souffle 136
Clam Chowder 44
Cleaver, Anita M. 107, 149
Cleaver Family 103
Columbus Inn 85
Cookies
   Applesauce Jumbles 130
   Chocolate Kiss Cookies 128
   Grandma's Sugar Cookies 126
   Magic Cookie Bars 123
   Red Raspberry Cookies 129
   Snickerdoodles 127
Cornforth, Doug 80
Courtney's 23, 24, 40, 79, 88, 152

Couscous Marrakesh 95
Crab
   Custard and Spinach Mousse with Sweet Yellow
     Pepper Puree 25
   Grandpop Ruoff's Crab Cakes 73
   Red Bliss Potato Crab Salad 35
   Seafood Quesadilla 22
   Shrimp and Crab Mousse Cakes 74
   Stuffed Mushrooms 18
Cranberries
   Cranberry Dream Bars 122
   Nana's Cranberry Mold 103
Cream Cheese
   Barb's Pumpkin Roll 142
   Chocolate Peanut Butter Pie 112
   Frosting 111
   Rosemary Ranch Potatoes 97
Cream of Broccoli Soup 41
Cream Puffs 119
Creamy Peach Pie 113
Crepes
   Nutmeg 141
   Strawberry-Ricotta 140
Curried Squash and Pear Soup 43

D

Davis, Lamont M. 16, 32
Deer Hash 67
Deviled Eggs 17
Dips, Chipped Beef 14
Dixie's Delights 133
Docherty, Arline 77
Doto, Janet 75, 128, 132
Durnin, Damian 65
Dyson, Linda 150

E

Eakin, John 139
Easy Chicken and Rice Casserole 53
Eggplant Parmesan 78
Eggs
   Christmas Brunch Souffle 136
   Crab Custard and Spinach Mousse with Sweet
     Yellow Pepper Puree 25
   Deviled Eggs 17
   Scotch Eggs 16
Elsohn, Neil R. 28
Exotic Mushrooms alla Bartolli 88
Exotic Mushrooms Angelucci 23

F

Fennel
   Blood Orange and Fennel Salad 33
   Gratinée 99
   Pot Roast Pork 66
Field Green Salad 28

Fig, Gorgonzola Cream 85
Fish
    Chilean Sea Bass Special 71
    Honey-Teriyaki Glazed Salmon 68
    Rice Paper-Roast Asian Salmon 69
    Veracruz 72
    Whole Roasted Black Bass in Sea Salt Crust 70
Fleming, Beverley Brainard
        45, 129, 138, 142, 145, 154
Frosting
    Cream Cheese Frosting 111
Frozen Bananas 132
Fruit Cocktail Cake 109

G

Gourmet Pancakes 138
Grandma's Pound Cake 108
Grandma's Sugar Cookies 126
Grandpop Ruoff's Crab Cakes 73
Gravy, Betty Ann's Mushroom Burgundy 153
Grilled Caribbean Chicken 57
Grilled Portobellos au Poivre 24

H

Hallowell, Jon 37
Hannum, Tom 36, 68, 74, 93, 153
Hawkins, Nan 96
Heart Scones with Blackberry Butter 145
Homemade Gnocchi 86
Homemade Goodies by Roz 143
Honey
    -Teriyaki Glazed Salmon with Asian Slaw 68
    Chilean Sea Bass Special 71
    Wild Rice 93
Hopkins, Robert R. 151
Hurd, Judy 46

I

Individual Cheese Cakes 116
Irby, Susan 126

J

Jerk Roasted Pork Tenderloin 65
Jerky, Beef 150
Jester, Shirley 34

K

Kipp, Cathy 78
Kledaras, Pete 66
Kwiatkowski, Jeanette 106

L

Lime Chicken 58
Little, Nancy 29
Little, Patrick 58

M

Macaroni and Cheese 89
Mackrides, William C. 60
Maddams, Barbara 127
Masseth, Becky 86
Matthews, Allison 94
McCartan, Cathy 43, 49, 84, 114, 154
McGonagle, Diane 73, 98
McKamey, Ann 17
Medisch, Leo 154
Mediterranean Cole Slaw 37
Medley of Vegetables 98
Melange Cafe 35
Mixmaster Café 37
Moro, Joe 71
Morrone, Colleen 76, 125, 153
Mrs. Habbersett's Orange Almond Buttercake 107
Mushrooms
    Betty Ann's Mushroom Burgundy Gravy 153
    Cape Fillet of Beef 61
    Caribbean Curry Chicken 56
    Easy Chicken and Rice Casserole 53
    Exotic Mushrooms alla Bartolli 88
    Exotic Mushrooms Angelucci 23
    Portobello a la Crème 21
    Quick Mushroom Soup 40
    Seafood Quesadilla 22
    Smokey Mountain Rice 94
    Stuffed Mushrooms 18
Mustard
    Brussels Sprouts with Maple Mustard Sauce 101
    Celery and Apple Salad Dijon 32
    Champagne Mustard Sauce 153
    Dijon Cream Sauce 52, 152

N

Nana's Cranberry Mold 103
Not-Just-Any-Chili Chili 46
Not-What-You'd-Expect Celery Salad 31
Nutmeg
    Crab Custard and Spinach Mousse 25
    Crepes 141
    Pregnancy Pasta 87
    Pumpkin Soup 42
Nuts
    Applesauce Jumbles 130
    Asparagus Cashew Rice Pilaf 92
    Frozen Bananas 132
    Magic Cookie Bars 123
    Nana's Cranberry Mold 103
    Orange-Jicama Spinach Salad 29
    Summer Salad for One 30
    Wild Rice 93
    Zucchini Bread 120

O

Ochenrider, Linda 113, 136
Older, Bob 21, 22, 33, 95, 144
Olives
    Cheddar Cheese and Olive Balls 15
    Fish Veracruz 72
    Spiced 148
Onions
    Becca's Blue Ribbon Meat Loaf 62
    Chicken Cacciatore 59
    Fish Veracruz 72
    Medley of Vegetables 98
    Splattered Chicken Pasta 60
    Vidalia Onion Pie 80
Orange
    -Jicama Spinach Salad 29
    Blood Orange and Fennel Salad 33
    Caramelized Orange Tart with Blackberry Puree 114
    Mrs. Habbersett's Orange Almond Buttercake 107
    Nana's Cranberry Mold 103
Orsetti, Eric 20
Outer Banks Gazpacho 48

P

Pancakes
    Buckwheat Cakes 139
    Finnish Pancakes 137
    Gourmet Pancakes 138
    Nutmeg Crepes 141
    Strawberry-Ricotta Crepes 140
Paris, Albert 69
Parker, Brian 61
Pasta
    Cheese Ravioli with Gorgonzola Fig Cream 85
    Exotic Mushrooms alla Bartolli 88
    Homemade Gnocchi 86
    Macaroni and Cheese 89
    Pregnancy Pasta 87
    Spicy Shrimp 76
    Splattered Chicken Pasta 60
    with Four Cheeses 84
Peach
    Buttermilk Soup 49
    Creamy Peach Pie 113
Peanut Butter
    Chocolate Peanut Butter Pie 112
    Dixie's Delights 133
Pear, Curried Squash and Pear Soup 43
Pennella, Judi 86
Peppers
    Crab Custard and Spinach Mousse 25
    Outer Banks Gazpacho 48
    Sweet Spicy Chili 47
    Sweet Yellow Pepper Puree 154
Philadelphia German Butter Cake 106
Pies
    Chocolate Peanut Butter 112

Creamy Peach 113
    Vegetarian Shepherd's Pie 81
    Vidalia Onion 80
Pork
    Jerk Roasted Pork Tenderloin 65
    Pot Roast Pork 66
Portobello a la Crème 21
Pot Roast Pork 66
Potatoes
    Casserole 96
    Clam Chowder 44
    Cream of Broccoli Soup 41
    Red Bliss Potato Crab Salad 35
    Rosemary Ranch Potatoes 97
    Vegetarian Shepherd's Pie 81
Pumpkin
    Barb's Pumpkin Roll 142
    Soup 42
    Toasted Pumpkin Seed Vinaigrette 28
Puree
    Blackberry 154
    Sweet Yellow Pepper 154

Q

Quick Mushroom Soup 40

R

Raisins, Gin 149
Rand, Amy 31, 87
Rawlins, Tim 52, 152
Red Bliss Potato Crab Salad 35
Red Raspberry Cookies 129
Rhubarb Crunch 121
Rice
    Asparagus Cashew Rice Pilaf 92
    Easy Chicken and Rice Casserole 53
    Smokey Mountain Rice 94
    Stuffed Chicken Breast with Dijon Cream Sauce 52
    Sweet Spicy Chili 47
    Wild Rice 93
Rice Paper-Roast Asian Salmon 69
Ristorante La Locanda 71
Rosemary Ranch Potatoes 97

S

Salads
    Asian Slaw 36
    Blood Orange and Fennel Salad 33
    Broccoli Salad 34
    Celery and Apple Salad Dijon 32
    Field Green with Toasted Pumpkin Seed
      Vinaigrette 28
    Grilled Caribbean Chicken 57
    Mediterranean Cole Slaw 37
    Red Bliss Potato Crab Salad 35
    Summer Salad for One 30
Salmon

Honey-Teriyaki Glazed Salmon 68
Rice Paper-Roast Asian Salmon 69
Sauces
Basic Marinara Sauce 152
Betty Ann's Mushroom Burgundy Gravy 153
Champagne Mustard Sauce 153
Dijon Cream Sauce 152
Maple Mustard 101
Sausage
Becca's Blue Ribbon Meat Loaf 62
Sausage Rounds 19
Scotch Eggs 16
Scallops
Rice Paper-Roast Asian Salmon 69
Seafood Quesadilla 22
Scones with Blackberry Butter 145
Scotch Eggs 16
Seafood Quesadilla 22
Shockley, Tara 18, 47, 67
Shrimp
and Crab Mousse Cakes 74
Bisque 45
Rice Paper-Roast Asian Salmon 69
Scampi 75
Seafood Quesadilla 22
Spicy Shrimp 76
Vieux Carré Scampi 77
Smith, Alice 108
Smokey Mountain Rice 94
Snickerdoodles 127
Soup
Clam Chowder 44
Cream of Broccoli Soup 41
Curried Squash and Pear Soup 43
Not-Just-Any-Chili Chili 46
Outer Banks Gazpacho 48
Peach Buttermilk Soup 49
Pumpkin Soup 42
Quick Mushroom Soup 40
Shrimp Bisque 45
Sweet Spicy Chili 47
Sour Cream Coffee Cake 143
Spicy Shrimp 76
Spinach
Crab Custard and Spinach Mousse 25
Orange-Jicama Spinach Salad 29
Pregnancy Pasta 87
Summer Salad for One 30
Splattered Chicken Pasta 60
Squash
Aunt Fanny's Squash Recipe 100
Curried Squash and Pear Soup 43
Sticky Chicken 55
Strawberry-Ricotta Crepes 140
Strouss, Kristin 14, 19, 53, 116
Stuffed Mushrooms 18
Sweet Yellow Pepper Puree 154

T

Taco Toss 64
The Dilworthtown Inn 70
The Hotel duPont 36, 68, 74, 93, 153
The Southern Mansion Bed & Breakfast 61
Toasted Bananas 144
Tomatoes
Basic Marinara Sauce 152
Bruschetta 20
Chicken Cacciatore 59
Medley of Vegetables 98
Not-Just-Any-Chili Chili 46
Outer Banks Gazpacho 48
Pasta with Four Cheeses 84
Tosh, Kristen 54, 133
Treese, Gerry 41

V

Valle Cucina Italiana Restaurant 20, 152
Van Name, Ted 48
Vegetarian Entrees
Cheese Ravioli with Gorgonzola Fig Cream 85
Eggplant Parmesan 78
Exotic Mushrooms alla Bartolli 88
Homemade Gnocchi 86
Macaroni and Cheese 89
Mushrooms Fra Diavolo 79
Pregnancy Pasta 87
Vegetarian Shepherd's Pie 81
Vidalia Onion Pie 80
Vidalia Onion Pie 80
Vieux Carré Scampi 77
Vinaigrette, Toasted Pumpkin Seed 28
Voss, Wendy K. 99

W

Waters Edge Restaurant 28
Webb, Dorothy W. 56, 72, 102, 148
Weischedel, Mark 110, 120
Whole Roasted Black Bass in Sea Salt Crust 70
Wild Rice 93
Wolf, Dale 42, 44, 100

Y

Yanek, Jonathan 85

Z

Zanzibar Blue 69
Zeigler, Jim 89
Zeises, Lara M. 81
Zucchini
Bread 120
Couscous Marrakesh 95

Order Form

Please send me _____ copies of Cooking with Goodwill at $12.99 per copy.

_____ Book amount

_____ Shipping fee

_____ Total amount enclosed or to be billed on credit card

Shipping: $3.00 for the first book; $1.00 for each additional book

Payment: Checks, money orders, and credit cards (Discover, MasterCard, and Visa) are accepted for payment.

By Fax: Fax this order form to 302-761-4649
By E-mail: Write to cookbook@goodwillde.org
By Mail: Mail form to: Goodwill Industries
                        Book Processing Dept.
                        The Goodwill Center
                        300 East Lea Blvd.
                        Wilmington, DE 19802

Ship to: Name _____

Address _____

City/State/Zip _____

Phone _____

Credit Card # _____ Exp.Date _____

Type of Card _____Discover _____ MasterCard _____ Visa

Name on Card _____

Signature on Card _____

Is this a gift? If so, to whom should we send it?

Name _____

Address_____

City/State/Zip _____

Questions? Call us at 302-761-4640 **Thank you!**